D1280248

Vitalizing Liberal Education

Vitalizing Liberal Education

A STUDY OF THE LIBERAL ARTS PROGRAM

by

ALGO D. HENDERSON

President of Antioch College

Harper & Brothers Publishers

New York and London

89565

378
1149½

VITALIZING LIBERAL EDUCATION

Copyright, 1944, by Harper & Brothers
Printed in the United States of America

All rights in this book are reserved.

No part of the book may be reproduced in any manner whatsoever without written permission except in the case of brief quotations embodied in critical articles and reviews. For information address Harper & Brothers

FIRST EDITION

A-T

LB
2321
H4

This book is complete and unabridged in contents, and is manufactured in strict conformity with Government regulations for saving paper.

To

ANNE

Contents

FOREWORD

By Ralph W. Tyler

Professor of Education, University of Chicago

A furious controversy rages over the future of liberal education. The wartime inflation of technological training with a consequent neglect of general education has intensified but did not begin a trend characteristic of higher education for more than fifty years. The necessity of readjustments in the post-war period makes the present an opportunity to re-examine educational purposes and procedures and to re-formulate a more valid conception of liberal education.

Mr. Henderson as president of Antioch College has had an unusually rich experience from which to examine the educational scene. For years Antioch College has pioneered in various educational innovations. Its educational program involves alternations between instruction on the campus and work experience in business, industry, agriculture, or the professions. The College has long recognized the importance of developing students who can relate the ideas and disciplines obtained in the several fields of instruction and can demonstrate their educational competence by passing an integrated comprehensive examination. Antioch has given more than lip service to its belief in democracy for the students and faculty together form a closely knit group jointly responsible for education and the general welfare of the college community. For the past five years Antioch College has participated in the Co-operative Study in General Education of the American Council on Education, a project involving the co-operative efforts of some twenty colleges and universities seeking to improve their programs of general education.

Out of this wealth of experience President Henderson has formulated his views on the kind of a college program which he believes to be essential for our times. This statement is not merely a reflection of the program of Antioch College but has been molded by his own intelligence,—the searching analysis that he has made of his observations of education and his consideration of short-comings evidenced in the work of various institutions. It treats not only the aims and purposes of a liberal education but also instructional methods, personnel procedures and community relationships. In a very real sense this volume presents the personal views of a thoughtful man with vision who has had an unusual opportunity for formulating his position. As such, this statement is significant and should be given thoughtful attention by all who are concerned with the improvement of the American college and the development of a truly liberal education.

Preface

AT A time when liberal education is most needed in the world, it is least wanted. A war-torn world needs the strength of leadership that liberal education can develop. It needs the pooled knowledge that can be derived from analyzing the experience of all nations, the tolerance and good will that comes with understanding the cultures of other races, the perspective that results from studying men's progress over the centuries, the wisdom that is distilled from the best philosophy of the ages. Especially for the task of reconstruction in the postwar world it needs this wisdom.

But for half a century the liberal arts curriculum has been losing ground, and for the duration of the war it has practically been discarded. It is thought of as a useless luxury which, in war terminology, is expendable. This paradox is explainable only by assuming that liberal education has failed—that is, it has failed to do more than play a luxury role in society.

Actually liberal education should have great social utility. I believe it does have. But I also believe that a new approach to this area of education is necessary if this result is to be achieved. Consistent with this belief, I have suggested a new definition (or orientation) and a revised content for liberal education in order to relate it functionally to life today. If it can be demonstrated that liberal education does have a highly important function in our dynamic society, there need be no fear that it will be displaced. I have attempted so to demonstrate.

A considerable portion of my discussion is devoted to methods. I have emphasized methods because it is important to show how the student becomes educated, and because the educational method used largely determines the results which flow from a philosophy of education. In improving their methods the liberal arts colleges have seriously lagged behind other educational institutions.

While writing this manuscript I turned for counsel to a number of persons in the field, and wish to express my appreciation to them for their help: George E. Barton, Jr., J. L. Bergstresser, Boyd H. Bode, Alvin C. Eurich, Louis M. Heil, Earl J. McGrath, R. W. Ogan, and Ralph W. Tyler; also to Dorothy Hall Smith for her generous assistance in the final editing. I am especially indebted to the faculty of Antioch College for helping me see fresh objectives and learn more productive methods in education. Since the book is aimed to arouse discussion, however, I assume responsibility for the ideas presented.

A. D. H.

Vitalizing Liberal Education

CHAPTER I

THE FUNCTION OF LIBERAL EDUCATION

ALTHOUGH the world is struggling through what may be the most far-reaching revolution of all time, liberal education, by and large, is sitting on the sidelines. The existing patterns in technology and in economic, social, and political life are being smashed and new ones forged. Human life has reached an acutely dynamic stage. And all the while liberal education, with its head buried in the sands of the past, is unable to recognize the tremendous forces at work and their significance in the march of human progress.

Even more tragic is the ineffectiveness of liberal education in producing leadership. Democracy, in the sense of the democratic selection of leaders and the democratic determination of policies, can exist without the benefit of education: e.g., as when a group of boys spontaneously decide to go fishing. But civilization can run downhill as easily as up. If democracy as the ideal social order through which to achieve freedom and equality of opportunity for all individuals, an abundant economy, and co-operation on a worldwide basis is to bring order out of the present chaos, it must have educated leadership. And the institutions of higher learning which pretend to give a liberal education should be the wells from which this leadership should mainly flow.

Liberal education, however, has its attention focused elsewhere. Its traditional purpose is the "transmission of the cultural heritage," which, as John Dewey says, is "a wonderful mouthfilling phrase."[1] Of course, there is nothing wrong with acquiring a knowledge of men's cultural achievements to date—that is, in one sense, the essence of education; but it is what one does with this knowledge that counts. It is right here that liberal education is socially impotent today. As Stewart G. Cole says: ". . . the fundamental weakness of the college is that it possesses no clear and commanding educational purpose to govern its policy, program, and leadership."[2]

The sterility of liberal education is implied in the very definitions given for it. Webster, for instance, defines liberal education as: "Education primarily for culture and by means of the liberal arts." Fowler, in his *Dictionary of Modern English Usage*, expands the definition to show more precisely what is meant: "It is the education designed for a gentleman (Latin *liber* a free man), and is opposed on the one hand to technical or professional or any special training, and on the other to education that stops short before manhood is reached."

The connotation is that of elegant leisure. "Gentleman" in the best sense of the term represents an ideal that is well worth striving to reach; but "gentlemen" who do not deign to soil their hands with productive activity or disturb their minds with vexatious contemporary problems are a luxury which the world is in no mood to afford.

---

[1] A symposium, *Educating for Democracy*, p. 139. Yellow Springs, Ohio: The Antioch Press, 1937.

[2] Stewart G. Cole, *Liberal Education in a Democracy*, p. 50. New York: Harper & Brothers, 1940.

The seriousness of this idea of education goes beyond the mere support of a luxury. The tendency has been to use a liberal education to maintain and to widen the class distinctions in society. This can be seen most objectively in the British system, where liberal education (qualified by some modification of policy in recent years) has been reserved as the privilege of the upper classes. The "school tie" has been the union card for admission to the Civil Service. The Civil Service in turn has held a monopoly on the policy-forming and administrative positions in the British Empire. The weakness of British policy in many parts of the world has been a natural consequence of entrusting authority and responsibility to men who have neither interest in democracy nor conception of what democracy means.

Liberal arts colleges in the United States have tended to ape Oxford and Cambridge. They have wanted their curricula to be unsoiled with anything contemporary, and in so far as they admit of vocationalism they have prepared students only for the "respected" professions. Thus their graduates are assured of social position and of white-collar jobs.

To make the criticism of the liberal arts college clear, let us consider an illustration that is admittedly extreme.

Let us picture a college that is wedded to the *status quo*. Its curriculum worships the past. To be cultural, a book must have withstood the test of time; literature does not become literature until custom has approved its style. It can then be read for pure aesthetic pleasure, the dross of social dynamic having refined away with the years. Adam Smith and Ricardo are still the wellspring of economic wisdom although their observations were made in the period of transition from mercantilism to the laissez-faire economics of the Industrial Revolution. And Thomas Aquinas is the saint who reveals God to the professors.

This imaginary college avoids any taint of vocationalism. A vocation is something apart from one's real life—it is the necessary but dirty business of earning one's daily bread, of producing objects which are sold in the market place. When a man is through with the eight hours of the day devoted to this kind of business, he can slip into his smoking jacket and consort with the great minds of the past, with only the glow of the fireplace to remind him of the world about him.

This college can comfortably avoid not only the market place but all the controversial problems of the day. Its professors can be scholars, who deal with ancient matters and supervise the preparation of theses on them. Their work is not designed to influence the sweep of current events. Thus the college can rationalize any apparent timidity in its leadership. There is no need for drawing into its policy-forming board the best creative thought of the lay occupations and professions, because the policy was formed in the dim past and needs only to be preserved. And the means of preservation are in a goodly flow of funds from wealthy contributors, whose dominant interest is in the *status quo*.[3]

In this kind of college, culture is acquired for its own sake, as a kind of veneer. Culture is a treasure to be hoarded, not an attitude that vitalizes and enriches life.

Although this illustration does not accurately describe

[3] This illustration and the one given later in this chapter have been taken from an article by the author, "Liberal Education in a Revolutionary World," which appeared in the *Proceedings of the Ohio College Association*, 1942, and in the *Antioch Review*, Summer, 1942.

the present-day college, it does represent something of its dominant emphasis. Presumably most college presidents approve of this emphasis, and it is the pride not only of the professors who are caught in their own cobwebs but also of the alumni, who for reasons of sentiment are hypnotized by the "treasury of culture" conception. The Bachelor of Arts degree stands as the sacred symbol; and the real definition of liberal education is once again revealed by the solemnity with which thousands of graduates each year are "admitted to all of its *rights* and *privileges*."

The only serious contemporary challenge to the liberal arts colleges has come from a university president. For several years Robert M. Hutchins has been raising his voice, castigating the colleges for their "vocationalism" and their lack of scholarship. "The college of liberal arts is partly high school, partly university, partly general, partly special. Frequently it looks like a teacher-training institution. Frequently it looks like nothing at all. The degree it offers seems to certify that the student has passed an uneventful period without violating any local, state, or federal law, and that he has a fair, if temporary, recollection of what his teachers have said to him . . . Little pretense is made that many of the things said to him are of much importance."[4]

It is unfortunate that Hutchins has chosen to attack the colleges on the one point where they have made some progress. Somewhat covertly, indeed, the colleges have been introducing vocational guidance services, and through some slight adjustment of the curriculum have been attempting to make education mean more, practically, in the life of the student.

[4] Robert Maynard Hutchins, *The Higher Learning in America*, p. 2. New Haven: Yale University Press, 1936.

They should be commended for this evidence of progressive thinking.[5] At the same time the colleges should recognize that while vocational adjustment is important to the student, and while the production of more skilled technicians, chemists, and accountants helps society to function and to win the war, the vocational program alone does not solve the main problems of society.

The remedies which Hutchins prescribes, too, seem out of focus with the needs of the times, and more concerned with administrative efficiency than educational advantage. For example, there is the proposal that the content of liberal education be made up of the great books of the past. The study of the march of ideas is, of course, tremendously important. But to suggest that these books be studied in a social vacuum sounds like suggesting that the colleges should burrow still more deeply into the sands of time. Then there is the suggestion that education should be stratified—"general education" being imparted up to the end of what is now the second year of college, followed (for those who continue in the university) by specialized study in the major and professional fields. Again, this suggestion has logic behind it if one considers only efficiency in curricular arrangement. But, if we assume that education is part of the life process, with the student gaining an ever-widening comprehension of the meaning and possibilities of life and ever-increasing effectiveness in living, the suggested curriculum sequences do not seem to be educationally efficient.

[5] See Algo D. Henderson, "Vocational Education in Liberal Arts Colleges," *Yearbook XLII, National Society for the Study of Education, 1943,* Part I, Chap. XXIV.

Hutchins' main point, that there be restored to the curriculum the emphasis formerly given to great literature, has genuine merit, but this idea has been more critically and constructively analyzed by the American Youth Commission. Although their statement refers to the high-school curriculum, it seems equally pertinent to the college level:

The traditional curriculum did have the purpose of passing on the culture of the past. This much is undisputed. What is forgotten is that the culture of the past, like that of the present, was not undivided in its search for the good, the true, and the beautiful.

As they found expression in the traditional curriculum, the classic studies actually had two objectives. In some cases, they did serve to bring young people to grips with "the deep, disconcerting issues of the nature of the universe, and of man's place in it and of his destiny." This was their great and enduring value. More often, however, the same studies in practice served no purpose more important than to provide mental furniture for the members of the professional and leisure classes in a society which was regarded as justifiably stratified, self-perpetuating, and relatively changeless.

Unfortunately, what is left of the classic studies in the high schools serves the second objective much more than the first . . .

The high schools must face the task of teaching in the field of life values and social ethics, difficult though the task may be. Moreover, if we are to be successful in teaching the principles of a moral order to the youth who crowd the high schools, we must recover the essential values of the traditional curriculum, but we must do so by providing subject matter and teaching methods that come to grips with the really great issues in terms that can be widely understood and appreciated. It is not impossible to deal with the greatest ethical problems in simple terms and with a multitude of homely illustrations . . .[6]

There are hopeful signs of progress through a re-examina-

[6] American Council on Education, General Report of the American Youth Commission, *Youth and the Future*, pp. 118, 119. Washington, 1942.

tion of the liberal arts program that is occurring in such experimental colleges as Bard, Bennington, Black Mountain, Olivet, Saint John's, Sarah Lawrence, and Talladega. And, also, Antioch. These institutions vary widely in their methods: Sarah Lawrence has successfully adapted to the college level many of the methods of the progressive school; Bennington, Bard, and Antioch have been using off-campus experience in varying ways to gain for their students a better understanding of contemporary culture; Black Mountain, Antioch, and Talladega make considerable educational use of the community life; and Saint John's and Olivet are using what might be called a semantic method of extracting meaning from the past. It is too early to appraise the educational results of these colleges in terms of outstanding contributions to the social order, but at least they are in their individual ways attempting to liberalize the liberal arts curriculum.

In spite of these evidences of new thinking about liberal education, by and large the colleges seem satisfied to follow the traditions of the past. They remind one of the bronze founder who is proud of having through years of hard apprenticeship learned how to cast statues in bronze exactly as Cellini cast them four hundred years ago. In the pride of his ancient art, he refuses to see the tremendous developments in science and in training methods which have taken place during the Industrial Revolution. Test one of his bronzes with an acid bath, and the holes in his work will be apparent. Similarly, the liberal arts college refuses to recognize the radical changes in educational philosophy and method which have been produced by the era of science.

Now a grateful world may well pay tribute to those

monasteries which, during the dark centuries in Europe, conserved the literature of Greece and Rome, and passed down the torch of education. In terms of the needs of their time, they were serving the most useful possible function in society. If in our own day the crazed notions of the Nazis should infect major portions of the globe, burning the books and preaching to youth the emasculation of learning, this function of preserving knowledge would again become a primary one.

But this attitude is defensive. Certainly we do not want to lose the benefits of the accumulated wisdom of the past. But the easiest way to lose them is passive hoarding; and the best defense for what is good in culture is to use it dynamically. If culture is valuable for humanity it needs to be spread more widely, and the wisdom of the past used to help advance the culture of the present. The attitude need not be that of saving culture from would-be despoilers. On the contrary, the whole of modern culture is in danger of disintegration from within unless the best wisdom we have is mobilized toward solving the crucial problems of the day.

Knowledge is dynamic. Through science we have acquired a new tool of learning, the method of analysis and synthesis. No longer need learning be imparted exclusively by indoctrination. Formerly knowledge was handed down from higher sources: truth was known, had been revealed, and needed only to be perpetuated. As long as this method was used primarily to transmit Christian ethics—which happened to have a great social utility—and to teach systems of communication and symbols for thinking, such as Latin and mathematics, the results benefited human progress. But the Nazi propagandists have well taught us that the technique of indoctrination is essentially authoritarian, and can be used as easily to promote the interests of a band of thugs as to promote human welfare.

The new way of learning is the way of exploration and experimentation. Truth is postulated, but not accepted as dogma. Through the process of analysis and synthesis, hypotheses are subjected to scrutiny and the conclusions tested by trial in practice. Thus new facts are discovered and principles refined and restated. Our knowledge of the ultimate truth is therefore relative to our immediate experience, which is part of the whole chain of human experience.

It is hardly necessary to remind the reader that as a result of the renascence in learning, accelerated so tremendously by the scientific method, knowledge has been expanding by geometric proportion. We are no longer limited to a little core of fact and dogma containing the essential wisdom of the race. The search for knowledge has been extended into every aspect of life. In the sciences alone, discoveries and more discoveries have been made—in geology, anthropology, biology, astronomy, physics—which have caused a complete revolution in thought. Witness, for example, the tremendous impact which the theory of evolution has had upon our view of history. Within the purview of our thinking have come whole new horizons of knowledge.

Man has available all the elements for the creation of a new era. With the coming of the age of science, knowledge became available as the basis for intelligent action. The fear of unknown consequences which fettered men's minds and bodies for untold centuries had been replaced with the possibility of confidence and courage. No longer need man be dependent upon the will and whim of his gods. He is free to search for and build the good life. William James's statement, "The world stands really malleable, waiting to receive its final touches at our hands,"[7] expresses the new attitude.

Furthermore, he has learned how to design and use tools of production with sufficient competence to feed, clothe, and house the peoples of the earth, and provide for all some measure of comfort and luxury; and to communicate this information within a matter of seconds to any spot on earth, and to transport the goods and services to any needed place. Only the barriers which he himself erects prevent this full realization.

This analysis suggests the new opportunity for intellectual leadership which lies before the colleges.

In an effort to make the criticism of our present liberal education more clear, let us imagine a second college, which can be contrasted with the college described on an earlier page.

This college has its attention focused on contemporary society. It encourages its students and faculty to study the world of living facts—in that world's strengths and weaknesses, major problems and trends. It makes firsthand observations of men in their daily work, and studies their aspirations. It spots the major pressures, and the pressure groups which are seeking to impress their needs (or impose their wills) upon their fellow men. It analyzes these pressures in terms of necessary adjustments and change. It aids its students to find their own best places in life, the places of greatest social utility, and to acquire foundation knowledge

[7] William James, *Pragmatism*, p. 257. New York: Longmans, Green and Company, 1931.

and skills through which to become effective in those places.

To help vitalize its policies, it brings in lay advice and experience from every walk of life—industry, labor, agriculture, and the professions. It reconstructs its policy as it goes in order to contribute to the most pressing needs of the time and to keep its curriculum vigorously alive. It seeks its income where current income flows, and fashions its economy to avoid depending completely for existence upon the accumulations of the past.

This college, too, draws heavily upon the past experience of men throughout history. But it does so not to seek culture for culture's sake but to shed light upon the present. Therefore it searches the past for wisdom that will help solve the problems of the present and will aid in planning for the future. This different purpose brings about a different method in teaching—research and analysis as opposed to recitation. The students begin their study with the culture in which they live, since they must understand it before they can try to improve it. To this college, culture is a process—life itself.

The acid test of liberal education should be this: What contribution does it make toward advancing the culture of our time? This question implies that the best contribution can come from those individuals who, attacking experimentally the crucial problems before the world, can bring to bear upon their solution the best thinking and experience of the past. These are the persons whom Harold Laski calls the intellectuals. "I mean by the 'intellectual,'" he says, "the man whose business it is to speculate upon the essential problems of his age. He may be artist or philosopher, physicist or mathematician, banker or trade union leader; so long as he is seeking to make the specialism in which he is involved a bridge from the particular to the universal, he is on my definition, an intellectual. It is my argument that his function is to assist in the understanding of the world we live in, that he may help the men and women of his time to a better control of that world, to , . . . therefore . . . the sense of a completer mastery of their lives that is implicit in that better control."[8]

In helping the intelligent young person achieve this goal, the liberal arts colleges should examine the culture of the present in the mirror of men's experience in the past and interpret it by the light of those values which have proved to be enduring or to have good social utility. This function applies throughout higher education and should not be confined to the liberal arts colleges alone. A "liberal education" is rather an attitude applying to the whole educational program than a set curriculum in a particular kind of college.

It is with the culture of their own day that the great thinkers, the philosophers and the scientists, of the past have always been concerned. Name any individuals you like —Plato, Augustine, Newton, Locke, Rousseau, Adam Smith, Darwin—the great thinkers of every generation have been concerned with the essential problems of their own times, and with the search for higher values in life, or for clearer truths. They blitzed through the encirclements around men's thinking and opened new horizons for exploration by men's intelligence. It is helpful to study Adam Smith not to learn contemporary economic theory—his theory written in 1776 applied to the problems of another revolutionary

[8] Harold J. Laski, "The Duty of the Intellectual Now," *Harpers Magazine,* Vol. 180 (December, 1939), p. 70.

period long since outdated—but to see how he analyzed and tackled the problems of his day. And in periods of radical change in the delicate adjustments of the social order, one gains perspective if he searches out the genesis of the change. For example, it is becoming increasingly clear that Karl Marx, Veblen, and Keynes, in their respective ways, have notably influenced modern economic thinking.

To put the whole problem in more specific terms: Thomas Jefferson had the notion that a wise society would search out its intellectually superior young people and give them the opportunity for higher education. To a people who are again taking great interest in democracy as a way of life, this is a pertinent suggestion. To prepare the best brains of a country for sound democratic leadership would seem to be a logical task for liberal education. Such a purpose for liberal education is both objective and functional. It gets away from the notion of trying to impose on the student "cultural" subject matter that is vaguely supposed to be "good for him." It gives liberal education a real part to play in society. It provides society with a good reason for supporting liberal education.

The ancestry of this function of training for leadership, furthermore, is respectable, being traceable back to Plato. In his model Republic, Plato put the philosophers of his day at the apex of the social pyramid and asked them to speculate upon the ways and means of making a more perfect society. Also, during and following the Middle Ages, the function of education was to instruct the clergy, whose function in turn was to lead the people toward the good life as it was then understood. Liberal education becomes nonfunctional only in a society where leisure instead of leadership has become the main interest of the privileged, and where culture has been made an artificial badge of social prestige. This is not to approve of the old basis on which leadership was determined, but in so far as education actually trained leaders, it was (though imperfect) alive.

The term "liberal education," then, today needs a new definition. It is an education that tends to produce the liberal individual—the person who, because of his perspective of history, his critical observation of contemporary society, and his understanding of social dynamics, helps to facilitate needed change in the world.[9] The function of liberal education is to help advance contemporary culture.

[9] Since phrasing this definition some time ago, I have noted the similarity of the one given by Cole: "A liberally educated youth will seek to conserve the priceless trophies of man's quest for the good life, to root out such conditions as inhibit every man's quest, and to make his own constructive enlistment in the cause of the common good." Cole adds this pungent note: "If the reader is inclined to remark that this conception of education is idealistic, the writer hastens to add that it had better be, for if anthropology has taught us one truth about man that is more significant than any other, it is that man is inherently a value-searching animal and a value-creating craftsman; and that very art of living has provided him with his highest value, intelligence. The only way to preserve intelligence is to use it to carry on the quest." *Op. cit.* pp. 62, 63.

CHAPTER II

THE COLLEGES NEED A VITALIZING PURPOSE

A CENTURY ago hundreds of new colleges, seedlings of the numerous denominational branches of the church, were springing up with dynamic resolve to carry the Christian faith and the best of Western culture to the common people. In 1862 the land-grant college movement, under federal subsidy, was instituted and in a few years spread throughout the country. From it surged a technological advancement in agriculture and industry which placed the United States far in the lead in the world in material progress. These two movements, accompanied by rapid growth in both public and private universities, were natural supplements to a greater one, the establishment of universal public education at the common-school level. With the schools came literacy, which Horace Mann promised would enable the newly privileged citizens to become intelligent voters in a democracy. With literacy came the craving for higher education. Through the technical schools, students were trained for service in science, and through the liberal arts colleges others were educated for spiritual and professional leadership. These are some of the reasons why America achieved its present strength and greatness.

Today the colleges (and to a considerable extent the whole of the educational system) seem confused both in purpose and in method. Their original spiritual drive has atrophied. To gain respectability and accreditation they have become conformists, scrambling for material assets. Their curricula have lost the unity which a clear purpose once gave them, and have become mere aggregations of departments. Following the lead of the universities, the colleges are becoming expositors of subject matter rather than teachers of students. Where once the liberal arts colleges through their graduates stamped themselves like a metal die upon the legislatures, the schools, the churches, and the professions, giving direction and purpose to a dynamic society, today they are in danger of becoming rubber stamps. I doubt if many colleges will, as is being predicted, fade away and die during the war period. They still have roots in the emotions of people, and in adversity they can live close to the soil. But the fact that the prediction can be made is evidence of their lack of any vital purpose.

Modern educators have got themselves into an introverted tangle about the purposes of education. Within the ranks of the educational philosophers have developed two broadly opposed schools of thought. There are the modern formalists who seem united in a determination "to free the mind"; and opposed are the progressive group who usually speak of "developing the whole of the personality." In method, the former advocate transmitting the cultural heritage of the past, and the latter start with a present interest or problem in constructing the curriculum. At the college level, this logomachy creates much confusion. Yet the meaning of liberal education should be clear enough to suggest a reasonably consistent approach.

First of all, the objectives of the two primary schools of

thought in education are not so far apart as their words seem to imply. Undoubtedly there is a wide difference between the conception of producing a "cultured man" and that of developing a "rounded man" who can succeed in living a satisfying life. The former goal is static; the latter, which is the newer approach, is less so, at least as far as the individual is concerned. The former assumes that knowledge or culture is worth having for its own sake; the latter, that it is a means to some other end—"to make acquaintance with the past a means of understanding the present,"[1] as John Dewey says. The first has its focus on the past, assuming that knowledge of the past is a prerequisite to a cultured life in the future; the second believes that the future is only the ever-continuing present, and that genuine education occurs only as the individual learns how to live to his fullest capacity now.

But each side has of late made some concessions which look toward harmony. Please note that the formalist no longer speaks of "disciplining the mind"; instead, he wants to "free the mind." And the progressive educator now seems to admit the need for some discipline if the student's interests are to take tangible form capable of orderly progression.

It is because the formalist wants to free the mind, and the progressive to aid the mind in achieving orderly development, that the objectives of the two are really not so far apart. "Freeing the mind" suggests producing an individual who is free to act primarily on the basis of intelligence and knowledge. And "development of the mind as one phase of personality growth" certainly suggests producing a person capable of applying intelligence to action. True, some formalists may

---

[1] John Dewey, *Experience and Education*, p. 94. New York: The Macmillan Company, 1939.

scorn the idea of character-building (for example) other than by developing the intelligence, and the progressives may argue that attention to other phases of personal development not only does not retard, but greatly facilitates, intellectual advancement; still, both are building upon intelligence. Is there any other way to account for the mad scramble for the top quartile students?

"Freeing the mind" is a high-sounding abstraction. What does it mean? If it means anything, it must mean the power to think. And if this is granted, thinking must be recognized as a primary objective of liberal education, if not of all higher education. And in so far as power to think effectively is a common goal of even different types of liberal education, it may help to unify their different methods and harmonize their approach.

For between the two basic philosophies there has long been a sharp difference in method. The formal method, in its purer form, relies upon inculcation. It preaches and lectures, admonishes and disciplines, enunciates doctrines and formulates rules. In an earlier day it secured excellent results. From the moralizations of the McGuffey Readers to the compulsory college chapel talks, from the drilling in the three R's to the fine points of Latin and Greek grammar, and from the dunce-cap punishments of the one-room school to the probations and dishonorable dismissals from college, the program of the formalists was consistent in theory and effect. Furthermore, the individual's whole environment—the home, the church, the village curfew, the apprenticeship system in labor—all molded the young person to the same end. He became a moral man, a literate man, a cultured man, who seemed to fit into the picture of his times as a disciplined and disciplining individualist. More recently, formal education has forsaken much of this technique, although it still relies on inculcation as an essential ingredient in method.

In contrast to the assumption that the student must learn a given body of knowledge, the progressive method starts with the individual, attempting to aid him in exploring his interests. It relies on activity or experience, directed by trained counselors, to secure change in the student—to make him something better than, and in some ways different from, what he was as a result of his previous environment and educational opportunities. It is the experiences of daily living that stimulate, temper, mold, and change the individual—experiences which the college can in large part shape. And by learning how to live successfully now he is prepared for living in the future.

Both the methods outlined above have their strong points. There is still room for argument as to whether it is advantageous to master a given quantity of background data as a preparation for the problems of later life or whether facts should be gathered as specific problems arise. It can still be urged that certain courses of study have been found through experience to be best in training the reasoning powers; or equally argued that no predetermined subject matter is so good for this purpose as that in which the student is already genuinely interested. Defining the goal as "power to think effectively" does not preclude teaching that the cardinal virtues are desirable in human life; nor, on the other hand, does it mean that direct inculcation of their desirability is superior to the method of so directing experience that the student may arrive at the same conclusions himself. On this last point, educators will of course disagree as to whether the cardinal virtues fall within the same category as two plus two equals four, but there will be little disagreement about their worth as subjects for educational consideration.

But there is no such thing as thinking in a vacuum. In order to develop the capacities of the students, colleges must provide them with something to think about. It is necessary to have a curriculum or a program of action.

The usual approach to determining what shall be taught is to consider what is *good* for the student. The formalist tends to rely upon the good old material which has withstood the criticism of generations. This body of knowledge, predominantly the classics, is the foundation of a liberal education. Human problems tend to repeat themselves (thus goes the argument), and the best approach in thinking about the problems of today lies in considering what past thinkers have contributed to their solution. Thus the cultural heritage becomes a springboard to the future. It is *good*, say the formalists, for the student to know this material.

Although the progressive has as one of his main goals the attempt to make the individual a social being, his approach, also, is what is *good* for the individual. He analyzes the student in terms of his needs and interests, and then starts working outward in concentric circles to develop the experience necessary to meet these needs and to enlarge these interests. It is desirable for the student to become a rounded personality; and consequently the progressive ends up with subject matter not too unlike what the formalist has provided for his students. To the extent that this is true, there does exist at the college level some uniformity of content for liberal education.

Neither of these approaches seems to possess a monopoly

on truth. If the curriculum makes no departure from traditional subject matter, the student will have—as far as the modern world is concerned—big gaps in his knowledge, and, conversely, will spend much time upon subjects the educative value of which is in question today. If a departure from tradition is made, the faculty scrambles to get the introductory course of each particular department included in the "required" list. The result either way is a compartmentalization of knowledge that tends to defeat the very purpose of a liberal education. On the other hand, if the curriculum starts with a particular interest of the student, there are all too likely to be permanent blind spots in those areas where the student has no interest to start with and where—so resistant to change is the human animal—not even skillful teaching can awaken interest.

Other weaknesses in the existing systems deserve attention. One is the separation, in the formal curriculum, of the "cultural" courses from those in the major field. This separation is usually accomplished by putting the general required courses in the first two years of college, and leaving the last two years to the field of concentration. There are objections to this practice.

Theoretically, under this plan, the subject matter is pyramided, with initial breadth of knowledge gradually tapering into some specialized field. There is logic in this, but the student doesn't live this way. He starts with certain interests, drives, and problems derived from his earlier environment, and broadens them at the same time that he is getting greater competence along particular lines. Furthermore, the usual curriculum varies from the "taper" theory by having the student complete most of his "cultural" courses before he can even enter upon his field study.

These cultural courses, prescribed because for some reason they are supposed to be *good* for the student, duplicate the secondary-school curriculum so much that they retard intellectual maturity; some of them seem bloodless and unreal to the student—and hence bore him at the moment when he is all eager and primed to do some work; they hang together badly because they are merely the introductory courses of the various fields; they invite procrastination and superficiality, and thus encourage habits and skills the opposite of the desired goal of disciplined thinking; and finally, this structure of general required courses is framed on the false assumption that a "cultural" education learned in the first two years of college provides the basis for living a cultivated and gracious life.

The failure to achieve pyramidal integration between the general and the field subject matter leads logically to two conclusions: one, that by the end of the sophomore year the student possesses the body of knowledge which constitutes culture, and thenceforth is finished with that phase of his education; and, two, that the cultural subjects are something apart from the field in which the person will spend his major working hours, and he must therefore, in college and throughout life, ride two horses with one foot on each. The separation fails to recognize that the individual has only one life to lead, and that his culture must be a part of his daily working and living, and not merely a veneer that embellishes the idle moments. This last conception is a carry-over from the old idea of a cultured gentleman.

The tendency of the present curriculum to encourage

habits of procrastination and superficiality deserves further comment. Such habits seem equally likely to develop from either extreme: forcing prescribed courses upon the student, or permitting him to wait until the spirit moves him. Effectiveness in living comes chiefly from good habits formed and skills learned. If we agree that education should get away from static goals and seek dynamic results, habits like procrastination and superficiality become serious handicaps. In inviting them we defeat the purpose of education. When formal education gave up its discipline through which prescribed courses were learned by rule, rote, and recitation, it was left with a conflict between purpose and method that has had many bad effects. When the progressive school depended upon the impulse of the student to determine the course of action, it lost the principal value which an educational environment provides. A school is more educational than other environments exactly in so far as it has planned its own environment to stimulate, counsel, and instruct students.

Another weakness in the average curriculum, whether formal or progressive, is that it does not develop rigorously the ability to think. In the formal type of education, the courses are informative, but handed to the student rather than used as the basis for further thought. And in the progressive curriculum, in practice, the problems presented are frequently of insufficient challenge to the students, nor is there required adequate collection and analysis of facts as a basis for arriving at conclusions. It is unfortunate for the one set of students that the method of research, once the only tool by which the content of a liberal education could be obtained, is no longer necessary—the factual information and ideas having already been discovered and neatly packaged as courses of study; and equally unfortunate for the second set, that the method of research is as yet so largely untried. Thinking is like other abilities in that practice improves the quality. Such techniques as making observations, and analyzing and synthesizing, need to become part of the student's working tools, with hypotheses and conclusions subjected to the criticism of skilled instructors. But present curricula are weak in their provision for these experiences.

Closely related is the problem of stimulating the appetite for learning, which involves many intangibles, and brings us to an area where earlier environment is a conditioning factor. Some people seem to have the spark and others do not. But a college will do little with the student if it fails to awaken and to broaden his interest. Assuming that college is but the introduction to a lifetime of intellectual growth, the significant thing at the school age becomes the *rate* at which the individual is growing rather than the *amount* of knowledge to which he has been exposed. It would seem, then, that the greatest effort to arouse interest or to build upon interest and expectations should be made from the start of the freshman year. Something more than dull or sketchy courses should be provided in that year; and here again, the method of research offers a kind of adventure and exploration that might help build up this appetite and maintain it. It is also possible that the system of grades and credits, based as it is upon time-serving and average performance, is not a fortunate educational device. It would be a revolution in both student interest and growth in capacity if, instead of requiring courses, grades, and credits, colleges were to set their requirements in terms of an individual's performance relative to his background and ability.

The chief reason for the weaknesses and compromises in American higher education is the narrowness of its objectives. To attempt to produce "cultured men" or "rounded individuals" without reference to the social scene in which these men will live and function is to create confusion concerning social purposes. Cultured for what? Rounded for what? In a nutshell, well-dressed for what? The significance of education must lie in more universal and more dynamic goals than these. In the eighteen hundreds the liberal arts colleges of the United States were not worrying about the handsomeness of their finished products; they were educating ministers, teachers, lawyers, legislators, and potential presidents. They were fighting to eliminate human slavery, to extend education to women, to bring culture to the uncouth Middle West. And they were venturing to explore the new theories of science, radical though these were in their conflict with the older theology which lay at the heart of the curriculum.

If the real function of liberal education in society today is to provide leadership for the progressive solution of the essential problems of society, then the education of the individual, including the solution of his own problems, gears in with something larger that gives it meaning. And the larger view is necessary if we are to get away from the present clutter and confusion.

Having liberal education serve this larger functional purpose helps to solve several difficulties. For one thing, it provides an objective beyond knowledge for its own sake. There is no longer a specific body of knowledge to be learned, and credit accumulations lose much of their significance. The past is searched for its facts and ideas, but is related in meaning to some end important to the searcher or to society. The student is then making common cause with the thinkers of previous times, who cease being cobwebbed volumes on the library shelves and become friends and counselors.

Thus does all pertinent knowledge become one. Knowledge ceases to be cut apart and tied up into bundles of required subject matter; and division of knowledge into "fields" can finally be recognized for what it is—a tool for convenient classification, filing, and reference. In working upon a specific problem of broad social importance, the student must draw upon such knowledge and methods as any and all of the particular fields have to offer. Integration takes place naturally as the student pursues his objectives.

This integration applies equally to the field in which the student may be concentrating his major efforts. For in addition to tackling an assorted group of the principal social problems of the day, the individual would just as now work intensively upon the problems of a particular area. There is no conflict between the two; they harmonize because they relate to the same larger whole. The major field is merely the place of the student's intensest interest, and the vehicle through which he probably will make his best contributions to knowledge and society.

Another important result is the way this approach integrates college with life. The principle that preparation for the future is best achieved through learning how to live fully and successfully in the present is accepted, but understood as referring to social values rather than to individual profit solely. The world about the student is his laboratory. The problems he considers are present and vital. The observations he makes are real. The conclusions he reaches have signif-

icance both in his own life and in that of the society of
which he is an integral part. The educational procedure followed is applicable in school or out of it, and hence as good
after graduation as before.

Furthermore, the experiences of the student bear directly
upon his educational growth. The importance of environment
as a factor in growth must not be overlooked. A college
should differ from ordinary environment in the way it plans
its environment to achieve the maximum of desirable growth
for the student. Campus activities, for instance, may teach
the student as much as, or more than, the courses of study;
but the teaching, undirected as it commonly is, may be good
or bad from the social point of view. Under the suggested
approach, the campus becomes a natural laboratory of living,
faculty and students together searching for a better way of
life.

Where the present curriculum often invites seclusion from
the workaday world, the proposed one makes observation of
and participation in the work of the world a prime educational ingredient. Off-campus experience—mingling with the
various classes in society; observing individual and group
motives, habits, and actions; studying production and distribution; analyzing industrial strife, community sanitation,
local politics, and what not—provides food for thought and
maturity of judgment. The resulting reactions and stimulation
can be put to good educational use.

An advantage not to be overlooked in this approach to a
liberal education is the spirit of adventure that animates it.
The expectations of the most alert freshmen about college
are met. College becomes a place with live people, interesting laboratories, and new experiences. The ideals which

many young people possess are here given opportunity for expression. The concern they have about the future, both for themselves and for their society, is the starting point for study. The curiosity natural to youth is allowed full play. The controversial problems—problems of religion, morals, politics, economics, imperialism, and so forth—familiar to all but puzzling to most of them, become open and free subjects of analysis and discussion. The faculty, rather than being spoon-feeders and disciplinarians, become counselors and fellow researchers. Out of this spirit of inquiry is struck the spark of motivation that "self-starts" the individual on the road to growth.

In terms of the individual, this approach produces the intelligent person who has learned how to bring his power for effective thinking to bear upon the vital issues of contemporary society. He may reasonably be expected to be truly liberal in thought and action; one who aids in making the transitions from existing institutions and methods to those necessitated by new ideas and developments if society is to progress. Aware of changing times, he has his emotional drive harnessed to reasoned action. The benefits, to individual and to society, are mutual.

In addition to offering the advantages just outlined, this approach serves finally to provide two points of focus for all systems of liberal education. First, if we assume again that a central purpose of education, irrespective of method, is to increase effectiveness in thinking, this conception of the function of liberal education provides unlimited opportunity to accomplish such a purpose. Every problem necessitates thought and involves every element and stage essential to disciplined thinking. Four or more years of directed practice in thinking thus give a reasonable foundation in skill and habit for continued future use. The educational experience can then be an ever-broadening one. In the second place, the approach provides a unifying objective around which to devise methods and determine content. The essential problems to be studied can be defined and their functional importance in society can readily be recognized. This does not mean that all institutions, or even all the students in any one institution, would be studying exactly the same problems; but even so, if this fundamental concept of a liberal education whose role is to produce leaders for contemporary society be accepted, certain major questions of approach and content will automatically have been settled.

CHAPTER III

THE SOCIAL INTEREST IN LIBERAL EDUCATION

SOCIETY'S interest in liberal education is in having it fulfill this function of helping promote human progress toward the good life. It is part of the function of liberally educated persons to help define what constitutes the "good life," and to keep redefining it from time to time as contemporary society changes.

Education must, however, take its direction from an over-all hypothesis concerning what constitutes the best society. Tentatively, the over-all objective of society might be to enable each individual to achieve the fullest development of his own personality and life consistent with, and at the same time capturing for society as a whole, the maximum values which can be gained from group association and endeavor. This formula is abstract, but it harmonizes the interests of the individual with those of the social group; it recognizes individual personality and also permits co-operative group undertakings. It fuses individualism and collectivism. Some such harmonizing process would seem to be the essence of democracy.

If we have not yet reached the perfect society—and the world revolution in progress today indicates that many think we have not—progress can be made only through change. Change implies the constant adjustment of our present aims, methods, and institutions to revised ideas of what is worth pursuing, having, and maintaining, in the light of new discoveries and new syntheses of experience. Negatively, this means the surmounting of obstacles to change; positively, it means intelligent search for desirable changes and putting them into effect. For society does not stand still, and the very goal we are seeking is that men should control and direct change by the use of their intelligence in securing reasoned action.

The great obstacles to freedom lie in the persisting demand for "absolutes" in aims and methods, the tenacious resistance on the part of vested interests, and the feeling of insecurity that comes from changing from the known to the unknown. The first of these is a carry-over from the period when because of ignorance and fear men leaned upon authority. Not understanding that experiences in life are relative and evolutionary, men sought refuge in absolute doctrines which promised security and salvation. The second obstacle represents the displacement of the greatest social good by the interests of particular members of society. These two phenomena frequently occur together, as witness the dictator who commands the adulation and demands the subservience of fellow men by means of vested economic and military power, accompanied by "revelations" of doctrines and decrees. The third obstacle, the feeling of insecurity, is in part the result of ignorance and in part a lack of commitment to social purpose.

All of this is not to say that there is no value in dogmas, or that our present accumulations of experience have taught us nothing. There are broad concepts, such as the test of the good society already enunciated, and still broader ones, such as honesty, temperance, and justice (what Plato called the cardinal virtues), to which we can relate particular actions and experiences and which serve as goals in our search for the good society. And in the use of the experimental method it is helpful to presuppose hypotheses and to search for verification in terms of "the ultimate truth." Undoubtedly, too, it is essential, if each new generation is not to start life from scratch in the evolutionary scale, to acquire and conserve the values achieved by preceding generations.

It still remains true, however, that freedom to change is the first requisite of a progressive society. The value of this freedom can best be seen through an illustration. Formerly men knew what was good because of authoritarian enunciations from those who professed to know. And the method of inculcation, in the hands of the fire-and-brimstone preacher, the moralizing teachers, and the paternalistic overseers of commercial and social activities resulted on the whole in well-disciplined individuals. But the result was a too-rigid system. For presently a big gap was discovered: the individualized ethics of this system was inadequate to cope with the new social problems brought about by a more complex and interdependent social scheme. Social morals, especially in the activities of modern organized pressure groups such as the legislative lobby, the big business corporation, the farm bloc, the labor union, and the totalitarian state, are still embryonic because only recent experience has revealed their importance. Furthermore, with the coming of scientific discoveries, future salvation was gradually discarded as an incentive for morality, and individuals became impatient with creeds as a whole. Young people, particularly, no longer would accept dictates of "good" and "bad," but wanted to test them by reason and experience.

This change in attitude has far-reaching possibilities. Society is being freed from blind adherence to the absolutes, which should greatly accelerate the process of experimentation for the good life. For educational aim and method, the point has special significance because of the expectations of young people, the relative effectiveness of experimentation as opposed to inculcation, and the greater vitality of an approach to education that is dedicated to social advancement.

These observations point to the importance of taking positive steps toward promoting change or, as stated above, searching for desirable changes and putting them into effect. This involves a twofold approach: speculation upon the larger purposes in life and critical analysis of the problems existing in contemporary society. Out of the two approaches must come plans of action which will attempt to solve these immediate problems in ways consistent with advancement toward the higher goals. Planning, as a technique in social progress, is here to stay.

The part which liberal education can play in advancing human progress can now be seen more clearly. It is exactly here, in facilitating these negative and positive aspects of change, that liberal education can make its great contribution.

The knowledge of men's progress to date should aid the student in several ways: in overcoming the fear bred of ignorance, in emancipating his thinking from the confines of dogma, in demonstrating how the *status quo* is but a step in the march of progress, and in giving him a stimulating acquaintance with the great philosophical thinkers in history. The knowledge which the student gains of his contemporary society should reveal its resources and its weaknesses, its more crucial problems, and the causes and sources of resistance to change. Finally, an understanding of social dynamics should give him an intellectual basis for his planning efforts and an emotional commitment to carry through to some worthy objective. An analysis of this sort makes these educative influences appear to be separable and discrete. On the contrary, they are highly interdependent.

The specific objective of the college, then, becomes producing persons with these qualifications. Its principal product should be leadership for society—not just any form of society, but the good society as conceived through some formula which liberal education itself helps to derive. A necessary concomitant, obviously, is to carry on at the college level a continuous exploration for the best way of life. This search, in turn, becomes the basic educational method and the spiritual fountain of vital leadership, both for faculty and for students.

Some additional discussion of leadership is warranted here. Leaders mean something more than those who march at the head of the procession. We obviously cannot educate leaders who automatically spring to the command. Leadership in any democratic group emerges from the rank and file of the membership.

Since society is dynamic, new pressure groups are constantly developing where inequalities exist. The leadership that emerges in these groups tends to be selfishly aggressive for the special interests of the group. Note how this happens in the younger labor unions. They resort, when the tensions become pronounced, to physical force. Perhaps they have to; but if so, it is because the leadership for both management and labor fails to see the larger social view. In the long run this method of determining issues is self-defeating, or at best highly inefficient for society as a whole. Democracy assumes a co-operative society, with adjustments among interests secured by intelligent planning.

Of course, leadership cannot be imposed upon pressure groups. Where there are pronounced inequities, as there have been in the labor field, the strong-arm type of leadership comes forward. The presence of these problems means that there has been a default elsewhere in economic or political leadership; otherwise the pressure would not come to an emotional head. The situation is in part self-relieving because as the pressure group gets concessions, it tends to reach a point where the margin of inequity disappears. At this point the pressure group must turn to a new type of leadership—men who can advance the cause by reason of facts produced through research. This would suggest that the labor unions, as they mature, will turn more and more to educated men for their leaders.

Leadership that is educated with an over-all view of society would seem to be the most desirable form of leadership. The colleges and universities, however, have been none too successful in producing this kind of leadership. Certainly in Germany the universities failed tragically; and in Great Britain the failure is likewise marked. In the United States the failure is only relative to what the success might easily be. In Germany the failure was due to intellectual remoteness from the common people; in Britain there was similar remoteness, due largely to artificial restriction in the supply of potential leadership material.

Two additional conclusions may then be drawn. One is that the potential leadership should be drawn from all ranks of society. Liberal education has been too much a class privilege. It was such a privilege in Rome, where education was available only to free men; it has been so in England, where higher education has been more or less the monopoly of the upper classes.

Even in the United States, studies[1] reveal that half the best high-school graduates cannot go on to college or university largely because they cannot afford to. In America, increasing discrepancies in income have coincided with mounting costs of obtaining a college education. The American Youth Commission studies show that two-fifths of all high-school graduates should go on to higher education, but only one-fifth do go. In the opinion of Homer P. Rainey, former director of the Commission, ". . . these youth who have the ability to go to college, but who do not go, are denied the opportunity of higher education primarily because of lack of economic resources."[2] The test of finances is not a suitable test in a democracy, where the guiding principle should be opportunity in proportion to merit. Yet it is the one we actually use. Even in the state schools, which during a couple of generations opened the way to college for most individuals of limited finances, growing costs coupled with

[1] See, for example, Herbert A. Toops, *Uniform College Information Blank Project*, Ohio College Association, 1935-36, pp. 2, 3, and 22; also, *The Prediction of College Going*, Table 12, p. 13.

[2] Homer P. Rainey, *Proceedings of the Institute for Administrative Officers of Higher Education*, p. 64. University of Chicago Press, 1939.

shrinking incomes close the door to large numbers of high-school graduates.

Our liberal education has been too preoccupied with advancing the social prestige of a restricted group of students. Our thinking has been in terms of leisure and luxury, and of white-collar jobs.

To a certain extent this situation is the result of an opinion that most people are uneducable. True, intelligence aptitudes of people vary widely, and hence there are wide differences in what people can best learn. But it is basic to the assumptions upon which a democracy rests that its citizens can make decisions derived from the rational consideration of issues. Fortunately, the whole of human activity proves that people are educable. The contention of uneducability, then, gets down either to narrow definitions, or to the rationalization of class distinctions. In any event there is no proof that the individuals with best intelligence come from certain levels in the social structure. Indeed, the contrary is clearly evident.

Here again, the Industrial Revolution—the impact of science—has changed the whole class picture. The need for literate workers and citizens helped bring about compulsory common education. With education, the capacities of the common people were demonstrated. With knowledge came the appetite for further knowledge. And through this process has come a certain vitality of leadership in American life, which has been lacking elsewhere.

The need now is to increase this trickle of leadership to a flow, by making liberal education available to all young people who possess the essential intellectual and personal qualities. The time is ripe for this action. In the war emergency and the world revolution that confront us, the need for developing this talent is urgent. We have become nationally conscious of the need for conserving and developing such natural resources as our forests and our soil; we need to recognize that the greatest of all our potential resources is our capable young people. It would be excellent national economy to make any necessary financial investment in the lives of these potential leaders. The growing complexity of the issues before the world and the expanding knowledge that must be mastered to deal with them requires the complete utilization of the ablest men we can discover.

There exists also a realistic reason for following this practice. The heavy immigration of non-Anglo-Saxon people that occurred during the nineteenth century introduced new problems of cultural assimilation. The more rapid birth rate of these people, and other minority groups, will bring added tensions in American life. It is essential to our "melting pot" theory, and to maintaining a successful democracy, that leadership be developed within all these groups—leadership of the type that liberal education can produce.

Consistent with this proposal, one phase of the Army-Navy Specialized Training Program should be commended. The students for this program are being selected on the basis of their records in objective screening tests. College courses are thus being made available to boys of a certain level of ability on individual merit. Lack of finances or social prestige is no handicap, since the government pays the full cost of tuition and maintenance.

The second conclusion about the education of leaders is that the education we give them must be related to the living realities of life. "Higher" education *ipso facto* is not enough

—it must be related to human values, must be for life in a democracy. In the light of the German experience, there is obviously the need of developing in students a concern for, and sensitivity to, the needs and aspirations of the common people. Leadership in a democracy should be for the advancement of the *whole* of society, not merely for special-interest groups or social cliques. The over-all view obtained through education, therefore, should include ability to see and desire to improve the whole, to understand the true breadth of the fundamental problems and to avoid superficial remedies. If students are to acquire this understanding, there is needed a far-reaching revision in the educational method of the typical college.

We must put some design into education for leadership. The tendency of the colleges and universities has been to produce, on the one hand, graduates who have a certain veneer of culture and, on the other, artists and scientists, specialists and technicians. Applying the veneer to the country-club type of boy and girl can be treated as a luxury item in society. The artists and the scientists are needed—and it is because genuinely competent ones are needed that the attacks upon "specialization" and "vocationalism" in the colleges can be regretted. To be productive or creative in any field of endeavor, a student needs enough intensive study in his field to gain real proficiency.

But something more than proficiency as technicians, economists, lawyers, and chemists is needed. We need persons who can work competently at specialized problems in their individual fields, but who can also relate their studies to achieving broader purposes in life. Society needs artists who can design, scientists who can create, social engineers who can synthesize human forces, administrators who can organize and manage whole areas in the social structure, and statesmen who can help shape the course of the whole of organized society—all building toward a better life on earth.

To promote this broader view can and ought to be the function of liberal education—the service which liberal education, as an element in the whole scheme of higher education, should render in a democratic society.

THE AIM OF THE STUDENT

THE service of the college to society is the primary justification for its existence. But a good society must be composed of good men; men educated for leadership in society must be competent individuals. It is therefore necessary, within this larger orientation, to consider how competence, effectiveness, and social-mindedness may be produced. The basic assumption is that the good society will allow individuals the fullest possible development of their potentialities in life. Students in the colleges are a picked group in ability: careful thought must be given to the proper cultivation of those abilities. And it is important to foster in students the highest possible aims in life. The dual objective in education—individual and social progress—is really a single one; in the performance of the social function of liberal education lies the best chance of satisfying the student's highest aims.

Granted sufficient ability, a student will progress in college proportionately to his motivation for learning. Motivation is therefore the key.

As Daniel A. Prescott has pointed out:

The final level of mental organization, the ultimate in attitudes for a particular individual, may be called his purpose, his *Weltanschauung*, or simply "what he wants to get out of life." Life may be lived primarily for the purpose of acquiring objects, power, prestige, or exhilarating experiences, and in this case the individual associates his welfare with materialistic factors. Life may be lived for the social good, and in the latter case, despite materialistic deprivations, an individual may feel himself significant as a school teacher, a government official, the manager of an effective business, as a soldier in a fascist army, or a farmer producing foodstuff. The essential matter is the orientation of his self-expression. If he feels that he is realizing himself best when he is doing something for the general welfare, it is because he associates his own welfare with the collective good. Self-interest still is regulating his attitudes. Finally, there is motivation on the basis of abstract concepts of good or beauty. For the glory of God, or for a moral principle which personal experience has endowed with strong affective value, a person may behave even to the detriment of his physical well-being, yet always for self-interest.[1]

Doubtless these basic drives are chiefly determined by environmental factors in early childhood, but in adolescence and at the college age the student is still susceptible to influences which may reorient, temper, or strengthen these motivations. Certainly the whole liberal arts program is founded upon that assumption. And right motivation is of fundamental importance if the college is to carry out its social responsibility.

There are advantages to the individual, also, in having his life adequately motivated. Unmotivated, he simply drifts with his environment. With definite motivation, he may become a productive and creative person. After rigorous examination of the subject, Prescott concludes: "All data show that adequate motivation is essential to genuine learning. No learning experiment is acceptable which does not

[1] Daniel Alfred Prescott, *Emotion and the Educative Process,* pp. 60, 61. Washington: American Council on Education, 1938.

take motivation into account."[2] It therefore becomes a first task of the educational institution to cultivate motivation in the student.

But measured in terms of social and antisocial values, motivation may be good or bad. Or perhaps a better way to express it is to say that motivation can be directed toward achieving a higher social culture or it can be indifferent to human progress as a whole. The direction the student is headed in is therefore of genuine concern to the college.

Some young people of college age already possess good motivation; many others are confused. That young people generally do not have matured convictions about values and goals in life has been demonstrated by the ease with which the dictators have molded them to their own purposes. If the student needs new or larger orientation in these matters, it is a function of the college to provide this orientation.

It is easier to suggest that this be done than to indicate how. How can the spark of action be ignited? How can the student be given a consuming desire to achieve good? There is not any one or simple answer. In part, the answer lies in creating an interesting, actively stimulating, and sometimes shocking environment, aimed at inducing educational change in the individual. Motivation toward fundamental values does not come overnight, as by conversion, but is a gradual development through successive and successful experiences.

There is, however, a place for influence. People are neither wholly automatic in their reactions to experience nor wholly rational in their actions. They are also emotional; and in part, students get their motivation by contagion. Any educator can think of vital teachers who have inspired their

[2] *Ibid.*, p. 179.

students to work toward great purposes. These teachers have not been coldly objective, rational, scholarly men. They have been creative men, who themselves possessed great motivation in life and were actively fulfilling their purposes.

Here, again, no formula will work with all people; and in any event we do not want to put everyone in the same groove. But it is reasonable to assume an over-all purpose toward which all men can devote their lives. And if this purpose is the highest possible one for men, it should also serve to induce the greatest possible motivation in college students.

What is such a purpose? For our day, it is the endeavor to improve society for all men. But lest the Hitlers lay claim to this same goal, there is needed some test by which to resolve conflicting values. This test can be whether a given course of action tends continuously to produce a social order in which the values are good will, understanding, mutual recognition of interests, reciprocity, and co-operation among men. The course of action that does so is good, and should have the right of way. Whether or not this is the ultimate purpose of life for all time, it is the one which stands the best chance of capturing the imaginations of the young people of today. They seem potentially to be socially minded. They are less concerned than former generations with personal glorification and ultimate salvation, with the goals of glory, power, and wealth. When they sense the maladjustments in society today, and the opportunities for creating a better life on earth, they respond with eager desire to participate.

It is in directing the student toward this end that the influence of instructors and counselors is important. Men of social vision, purpose, and action can contribute tremendously toward giving the student a vital sense of direction. Because the college faculty is itself limited in experience and wisdom, it is important also to extend the contacts of the student with men and women who are active in world affairs.

The way that this larger aim of the individual student coincides with the function of liberal education is apparent. They are one and the same.

The hope which science has brought to man is that man is able to create not the world itself, but an increasingly better life on earth. In spite of catastrophic wars and serious social maladjustments, the prospect is encouraging.

To the individual, science has brought a new kind of personal significance. His potential status has changed from subject to freeman; from dependence on natural and social forces to mastery of the natural and determination of the social; from action dictated by authority to action based upon reasoned judgment. As a potential fellow creator of the society in which he lives, the individual gains self-respect and self-confidence. Thus he comes to his full stature as a human being. Thus he helps achieve for his fellow men a higher level of culture.

The individual's expectation is to achieve the fullest expression of his personality, which seems to be the natural goal of individual life on earth. This expression should be in line with his interests and abilities, as determined by his own choice. But since theoretically the best society can come only through having each individual make the finest contribution of which he is capable, it is to society's own interest to devise ways and means of discovering the individual's distinctive capacities and talents, and of enabling him to develop them. Through this process, the individual, too, uncovers new possibilities, and his interests expand in the direction of his greatest potentialities.

Expression for the individual implies freedom. Essential to that freedom is the creation and maintenance of a social organization that permits the maximum individual advancement consistent with the greatest common good. The basic difference between a free society and one which is not free is the respect maintained for individual desires, talents, and differences in personality, while at the same time the group strength and resources are utilized to achieve a social environment beyond anything that individuals working singly could realize.

. . . . . .

If we grant that the education of the individual student should be oriented to the over-all purposes of a personalized society, there still remains the problem of counseling him concerning his own individual objectives in college. This counseling, obviously, should be based upon the fundamental assumptions underlying the educational program as a whole. Personal advising is an individual matter; but the following outline suggests the kind of analysis which can be made:

First of all, one objective of the student should be to enlarge and mature his interests. To help him define his interests and determine his aptitudes will be the point of departure in counseling any student. These interests and capacities may be tentative—presumably they will change and grow considerably as time goes on—but there is distinct value to him in setting up tentative goals and in making tentative appraisals of himself.

Failure to discover and define interests leads to waste and often to tragedy. Failure to define interests while in college handicaps the student in two ways: he fails by that much to get an adequate preparation for his lifework; and—of more importance educationally—he must pursue his studies without the motivation and drive that come from aroused interest.

Determining on his lifework is an immediate concern to every young person of college age. Individuals must have some means of subsistence, and ordinarily the daily work a man does is also the medium through which he makes his greatest social contribution. As his work progresses from elementary stages to more complex, it may also become a main avenue for self-expression and for securing happiness. It is unfortunate that the word "vocational" meets such an unfriendly reception from college faculties, because the occupational adjustment and training of young people is an important need both to them and to society. If we define "vocation" as the lifework of the individual, the truth of this statement becomes evident.

The difficulty too frequently lies in a failure to discriminate how much emphasis to give the vocational element. Too often the assumption is that a program must be either wholly vocational or wholly cultural and liberal. From the student's point of view, however, it should be neither the one nor the other. If the principle of developing the individual's own best talents is followed, then there is at certain levels a place for educational programs largely devoted to manual and physical training, and equally a place for programs aimed primarily at intellectual development. But the important thing in *any* program emphasizing vocational training is to weave into it as much of the liberal curriculum and point of view as the students can assimilate. This is essential if we are to gain the larger social objectives of a democracy; it is essential in educating for citizenship. Conversely, the important thing in the liberal arts program is to include in it sufficiently specialized and diverse fields of interest so that the student may gain basic knowledge looking toward his particular lifework. Stated another way, the concern of the educator should be with the proper balance between the vocational and the liberal at different levels and in varying kinds of institutions, since both elements are needed in every curriculum.

Along with the vocational interest, the individual needs to acquire and broaden, and learn how to make effective in his life his avocational interests. Interests of all kinds are so often determined by environment and chance that more often than not the student's interests when he arrives at college are narrow and inconsequential. While he is still in his formative years, he should be encouraged to seek interests which will aid that whole personal development necessary for the best life for himself and his society, particularly since modern life has provided so much leisure time. Leisure time is not a time for idleness. It is a time for fun and recreation, for productive and creative activity, for work that helps build the more perfect society.

A second major objective of the student should be to develop greater personal and social effectiveness. Of obvious value in leading an effective life is health, both physical and mental. It is apparent that the individual needs some skills of thought and action, such as the ability to think analytically and to express himself well in writing and speaking;

and those who have special talents of imagination, calculation, manipulation, or physical dexterity should be helped to perfect such techniques in design, mathematics, invention, research, or in the arts and sciences generally as will give them the personal fulfillment that is part of the aim of education.

But beyond this, the individual needs to develop those personal characteristics which aid him in his relations with other people. The modern man is an integral unit in a complex society. He would quickly perish but for the assistance of others; more positive is the need to acquire social effectiveness in order to fulfill his own highest aims in life. A co-operative society demands good will, tolerance, and a spirit of give-and-take. The individual needs faith in himself, which comes from understanding his own limitations and possibilities. He needs also an understanding of the society of which he is a part, and a commitment to working toward the more perfect society. In brief, he needs not only an intellectual understanding of the cardinal virtues of wisdom, temperance, justice, and courage, but needs also to learn how to make them motivate, govern, and vitalize his life activities. And he needs to acquire social skills in working with other people and in organizing and directing others toward group objectives.

To be effective, too, the student needs to acquire knowledge and skills in the field he has chosen for his lifework. If his choice is journalism, for example, obviously he needs training in writing. But he also needs to study more intensively in those areas—economics, sociology, government, psychology, literature—which will best help him to interpret the events about which he writes. And he should try his hand at journalism to test his competence, for unless he shows promise of competence he should transfer to some other interest.

In advising the student, the counselor should emphasize and encourage him to develop creative habits and skills. College programs tend too much to promote passive habits, to foster the spectator attitude. Students are lectured to; and when they discuss, they talk *about* things without experiencing the values they attempt to measure. Their music, their dramatics, their athletics, are geared to the spectator interest, and all but a handful of students sit and watch. Education would be more fruitful if the emphasis were put upon planning and participation. The student should be taught the habit of creative planning—concerning his health, his economic status, his leisure-time activities, his social environment and pursuits, and so forth—and should cultivate the habit of productive work in his individual interests and of creative participation in his community life.

The student's third objective should be to enrich and mature his philosophy of life. An individual's conception of his life aims grows with time and experience. But the college period, coming at the threshold of such major responsibilities as marriage, citizenship, community relationships, and an occupation, is an especially suitable time for the consideration of life's meaning and objectives. If the individual is to achieve the personal distinction that is his right, he needs to get started toward this end. If society is to have his assistance in moving toward more satisfying goals, more universally applicable principles and methods, he needs as an intelligent member of this society to formulate his own relation to these goals and to gain social-mindedness and social motivation. While maintaining an open mind toward the whole of human progress, so as not to stultify his perception of new truth, he needs to be able to act toward human welfare as well as contemplate it.

In part, this means that he should seek freedom from inhibiting influences. For example, while aiming at reasonable economic security, he should develop an over-all philosophy that will enable him to take or change jobs, to marry, or to undertake civic activities, in accordance with his primary goals in life rather than for economic security. Similarly, he should free himself sufficiently from fear of losing social prestige to enable him to voice opinions or to fight for unpopular causes and values in which he believes.

All these objectives can be accomplished by acquiring a comprehension and understanding of one's human and physical environment; and especially can one develop a philosophy of life this way. The student should come to see himself, in perspective, in relation to the history of the earth and of the people on it. The way our present culture is founded on the cultures of the past is significant to the person who will be a creative factor in the present culture. Thought, inventions, discoveries, customs, mores, and habits are all cumulative in their bearing and effect. Man's relations with his fellow beings are both in space and in time. Territorially and qualitatively, the student needs to have his knowledge and understanding of his contemporary culture widened far beyond the narrow confines of his earlier environment. In part, this means an acquaintance with the physical and natural sciences: man needs to know the extent to which he now can be master over natural forces. In part, also, it means analyzing what men think or have thought to be good aims in life, in order to help determine toward what ends the student will attempt to use his mastery.

The objectives outlined above, of course, are not separate or mutually exclusive. Indeed, vocational and avocational interests, and personal and social effectiveness, are but integral components of the philosophy of life. They are the channels through which that philosophy receives expression and meaning. All together, they represent the coupling of emotional drive to reasoned action.

Naturally, many of these bents have been "set" by environment and previous education before the student reaches college. Likewise, experiences after college influence the individual's goals and progress. But the immediate objective of college education is to produce change and secure growth in the student. And the way to do so lies in analyzing with the student his fundamental and developing aims.

CHAPTER V

KNOWING AND ADVISING THE STUDENT

THE college has no magic wand to turn students into educated men and women. Even though it may get them to the brink of knowledge, it cannot make them drink. The legal power to issue diplomas is not necessarily the capacity to educate.

There is nothing mysterious about an educational institution. It is but a planned environment in which the individual will live and work temporarily—planned to give the student greater opportunity for personal growth and social maturation than he would find in the environment of chance. The initial planning of this environment must be done by the faculty.

We have assumed as the ultimate objective of the good society an equation between individual advancement and social progress. The individual has as his due from society the opportunity to develop his own personality to its fullest potentialities. The individual is the medium for the educational effort. Such change as occurs will occur in him. Results achieved can find expression only in his life. The group can be different from and greater than the sum of its parts, but the values must be derived from the individual units. Education has to start with the individual.

It follows that the college should know its students. This

means something more than greeting the freshmen at a college mixer or entertaining students in faculty homes. The knowledge of the individual that comes from personal or intimate relationships is valuable; indeed, it is indispensable. There should be more rather than less direct personal acquaintance with students. But in itself this acquaintance does not produce adequate knowledge about the student, for the reason that the observations made of him under these circumstances are neither objective nor thorough. Frequently they do not go beyond the immediate social situation. And, of course, in an institution of large enrollment any social affairs or efforts at entertainment will usually be superficial and perfunctory. In short, personal acquaintance with students, important as it is, does not alone satisfy the need of knowing them.

The better the college knows its students, the better the educational job it can do, for planning and doing the job depend largely upon understanding the material there is to work with. The individual for his part can hardly hope to achieve his greatest potentialities unless these have been discovered and his interest in the possibilities has been stimulated. This understanding should include all phases of personality development, an analysis of which has already been suggested under the headings of vocational and avocational adjustment, personal and social effectiveness, relation to human and physical environment, and aims and driving power in life.

The aim of teaching is to help the student grow: to assist him in improving his capacities for observing, thinking, discriminating, and acting—for making his best contribution to society. The student must be aided to educate himself.

This concept of teaching differs radically from the older method of securing the desired results through discipline. The latter presupposed specific subjects which were good for the student, which would discipline his mind; specific moral codes to which he must subscribe and which limited his actions. There were arbitrary standards of achievement concerning subject matter alone, which had no relation to his own abilities or progress but which measured his "success" or "failure." It was a system of artificial incentives, inculcation, and rigid discipline. It was weak at the outset because it neglected to secure the full co-operation of the individual. The road led to notable successes, but it also was strewn with maladjustments and failures.

Grade-school pupils are no longer whipped for their failures, but college students are still commonly subjected to punishment not different in principle from the dunce cap. Only a few institutions have discarded the method of probations and dishonorable dismissals; and some still require physical labor of a student as a penalty for the infraction of college rules. Fewer still have given up disciplinary lectures and tongue-lashings. These devices may be the easy route to apparent administrative efficiency, but they are hardly the approach to aiding the student in finding and working out his potentialities. Can punishment for ignorance, incapacity, lack of discrimination in social values—for emotional instability, physical handicaps, lack of interest in imposed curricula, poor habits of concentration and application, or lack of essential skills for thought and expression—possibly be justified as the best educational device? And should the faculty be content with less than the best approach to the solution of the student's problems?

This statement might be taken to imply that it is the primary business of the faculty to deal with problem cases. Too often in counseling work the "problems" are the limit of the effort made—frequently, for sheer lack of time. But, although lack of time is a plausible excuse, the result is that the college fails to do its best job. The students who are normal in their abilities, habits, and general reactions to the college environment and the students who relatively have the greatest intellectual capacity are the real justification for the educational program and expenditure. The deficiencies and maladjustments of the problem case should be cared for—frequently the task should be transferred to another agency such as a mental health clinic. But all students deserve the same positive effort, which means that the normal and superior students should receive their full share of educational guidance and instruction. In any event, the negative approach implicit in the older disciplinary method more often than not fails to accomplish the desired end. Punishment makes an impression, but it may be a different one from the impression desired. Teachers should not be hurdles in the path to progress; their natural function is to stimulate, counsel, and instruct.

A first essential, then, in effective teaching is to know the student. As indicated, this is only partially a question of personal acquaintance. It involves as well the accumulation of objective information about the student. The doctor takes a case history of his patient, the lawyer builds a brief as he analyzes the case of his client, and the research chemist is a long way on the road to a solution of his problem when once he has it clearly outlined and defined. Should the teacher be any less scientific and methodical in the objective phase of his approach?

Parenthetically, it may be mentioned that analyzed facts about the students and the kind of environments they come from are of great use to the college when it plans the institutional program.

Getting the requisite knowledge about a student is a process of observation and accumulation of information. The first step is to determine what information is pertinent and should be collected. Collecting information cannot, for financial reasons, be an institutional hobby. Nor is the primary purpose to preserve information for chance use by future generations—although there is historical value in records. The purpose is to aid the individual student to get the best value from his time with the college, and to assist the college in planning and working toward this end. Historical information is the basis for present action.

Most of the information to be sought will be common to all students. That is, the questions can be the same; the answers may vary widely. This makes it possible to develop general criteria which save time and effort, and which are useful in making comparisons and thus arriving at relative standards of abilities and accomplishment. Since a given institution must define its particular purposes and scope of work, some of the information desired will apply to its own special needs. If the curriculum is a limited or special one, for example, special attention will be given to aptitudes and interests consistent with the program. If a set of criteria for advising the students is first formulated, the particular information which should be obtained becomes more apparent.

Often the answers to the general questions will suggest special ones for the particular student.

The college has first of all to determine whom to admit as a student. Parenthetically, since the college must also reject students who presumably cannot profit from its program, the information collected aids in suggesting to these rejected students some better plan for them. Securing the information essential to a selective admissions policy serves a dual purpose: admission, and securing the basic case history which starts the college personnel record. There is no inconsistency in these two objectives, but they should both be borne in mind.

The information desired will normally include a brief family history, noting especially such environmental factors as unusual cultural associations, special flairs or talents, friction in the home, and abnormal health problems; the community environment, again with special note of cultural associations, civic attitudes, and access to books and laboratories; the secondary-school record, both of academic work and of activities; the experience record outside of school; the individual's health history, including a present examination; and the observations of parents, friends, and teachers concerning personal characteristics, abilities, and motivations.

A self-analysis by the applicant (possibly in answer to leading questions) may be revealing about habits, good or bad, maladjustments, skills of thought and expression, and aims in life. In addition, it will be desirable to confirm the conclusions drawn from these observations and records by giving the individual tests of intelligence, specific aptitudes, academic achievement, personal adjustment, and health knowledge and habits. With such information available, there is a basis for making a reasonable guess about a student's capacity to profit from the college program, and whether it is worth society's time to give the individual the opportunity.

If this information has not been obtained before admission, it certainly should be accumulated as soon afterward as possible. Effective advising is difficult unless the counselor has available from the start adequate information with which to work, and to gain the student's interest and confidence. Preliminary facts are important, although they will be supplemented both in quantity and in interpretation by the initial conferences. Part of the college record will be the observations, skilled or common-sense, noted by these advisers.

The type of information suggested as a start for the personal record should continue to be collected. The day-by-day and year-by-year record of the student should include observations on the growth of the whole personality, rather than be limited to the strictly academic, plus references to disciplinary encounters. And this implies not only records of activities, experiences, and achievements—academic, vocational, and social—but the results of such repeated tests of progress as it may seem wise to give. Aptitude or personal adjustment tests may be worth giving a second or a third time, especially in the light of new evidence or new observations about the student. Since the student's apparent "intelligence" can improve considerably in a favorable environment, it is important in counseling not to rely on the initial test results alone. If class examinations are given in the separate courses, tests of total achievement and of residual knowledge are valuable, as are also broad tests of the student's ability to apply his knowledge to important social problems. Additional self-analyses, given not so often as to cause undue introspection, are interesting ways for the individual to check his own progress and redefinitions of his objectives. Annual physical examinations are excellent both in college and as a lifetime habit.

Not least valuable is the record of the trial-and-error process in vocation-finding, social adjustment, and the acquisition of skills. For education is achieved only when progress in these areas is included. The record helps "stake out" that progress, not for the sake of determining when the diploma is due, but rather to locate errors and miscalculations, to indicate new directions for trials, to avoid unnecessary repetitions and circle-chasing, and to permit progress to accelerate as experience accumulates.

Since the whole student is the concern of the institution, two further observations are pertinent. One is that to help avoid diagnosis and advice from isolated or too superficial or subjective evidence, the record of each student should be put together into some sort of whole containing all the information collected about him. A good practical form is a central record card, on which all information is briefed, supplemented by a folder giving the elaborations and details. The other observation is a qualification of what has been said. The emphasis in education should be positive rather than negative. In addition to the course grades and credit-hours, academic records typically concentrate on the blemishes in the student's life at the college; there is merit in the contention that these blemishes should be erased from the record when the student has overcome the difficulty. Much harm can be done the individual by emphasizing these incidental failures. This is a form of perpetual punishment not unlike branding the one-time convict for life. It is the possibilities in human personality, not the limitations, that are the educational and social goal.

Some of the uses to which knowledge about the student may be put have already been indicated, but a few further points can be made. For one thing, the information must be made available to the faculty and there must be some organized means through which the counseling can function. Availability again means records for use and not for history. This does not imply that the personal information noted on the central record should be accessible to any curious inquirer. The answer does imply a quality of advising service which the college does not always possess.

The counseling of students is a professional aspect of the profession of teaching. It deserves the attention of interested and thoughtful, and to some extent trained, persons. If the counselor does not himself possess a matured outlook on life, breadth of knowledge, personal enthusiasm and commitment to high individual and social purposes, how can he stimulate the student? And if he does not possess skill in his relations with other people, in his ability to analyze problems, to induce thinking, and to project possible solutions, how can he counsel to best advantage? Further, if he is not always ready and willing to grasp experiences of the moment that may stimulate the student to improve his knowledge and prepare better for future action, how can he do the teaching that is inherently possible in his relationship with the student?

The counseling setup deserved by the student body is somewhat different from the usual dean-of-men and dean-of-women system. Unfortunately, the tradition of discipline surrounds the titles and the work of these officers. Frequently the dean's chief qualification is that of being a good fellow— he can discipline and get by with it. Too seldom has he had genuine personnel training. Often, too, his own staff is so small that it is hopeless for him to attend to any matters excepting those which crowd upon him. He must then handle these in the shortest and quickest way possible—which, with students, is to suppress or dismiss them. Administrative discipline and counseling tend to conflict and therefore need to be tied together skillfully if they are tied at all.

And when the faculty have not been sensitized to the educational opportunities in a carefully planned counseling system, they may respond with scant enthusiasm, do only the necessary registration-clerk duties, and undermine any possibilities in the work by nullification and sabotage.

It is not necessary to have a staff of counselors completely distinct from the teaching faculty. This would be a mistake, for the reason that counseling should be about the facts and activities of everyday life, a substantial element of which is the academic program. The ideal counseling service would be integrated with the program as a whole by being a natural by-product of the educational process; the ideal faculty would fulfill the threefold teaching function of stimulating, counseling, and instructing. It may someday become the tradition in college teaching that the faculty shall have interests and qualifications for their work in addition to professional attitude and training in their academic fields.

It is, however, advisable to have specialized counselors in certain areas. The general faculty advisers need to train themselves for their functions, but certain problems in personal development are too technical for them to consider handling—for instance, health, both physical and mental. Illnesses, physical handicaps, and emotional disturbances need the skilled observation and treatment of the health specialist. To this, all would agree. It is not so obvious but is none the less true that specialists in many other skills, including library usage, laboratory techniques, speech and writing, reading methods, and so forth, can greatly expedite the learning process.

These specialized problems need both careful and positive handling. To illustrate, it is a natural phenomenon for young people to fall in love. Lovesick couples are frequently oblivious to the work of the day, and thus a drag on the institution. The disciplinary remedy brings no genuine or lasting solution, especially when the boy and girl are under the jurisdictions of separated deans' offices based on sex differences rather than on difference of function. The soothing sympathy of the average members of the faculty stands as good a chance of aggravating the situation as of solving it. It is apparent that there is needed a counselor who, because of adequate understanding of the psychology involved and of the emotional tensions which exist can reach the confidence of the individuals and convert a negative situation into an educational opportunity. The same reasoning applies to the boy who because of pimples on his face feels inhibited from participating in group discussion, or the student who, coming from a background of fundamentalism in religion, becomes bewildered and confused when he studies anthropology or evolution, or the individual who, because his eyes will not focus, fails in courses with heavy reading assignments, or the boy who because of a conflict with his parent over vocational aims fails to make progress in his selected field. The positive solution of problems like these frees the individual for effective work.

The use of specialized counselors does not relieve the general adviser of all responsibility. Upon him will normally fall the first-aid task of diagnosing the possible causes of difficulties. He must have sufficient awareness of the possible relation between personal maladjustments and the student's failure to make the progress of which he seems capable. Of equal importance, he must know when to refer the case to a specialist instead of trying to handle it himself. On the other hand, he must avoid the creation, through wrong handling, of problem cases.

The value of having the specialist understand the general educational problem and integrate his work with it is not always stressed enough. To repeat, the student is a whole. His best development does not come from the sum of numerous specialized treatments. Each special problem needs to be considered in the light of the individual's whole growth; and the study of the student as a whole can best be undertaken only when the knowledge of the specialist is available in the general picture. The rare exception may be the situation where a basis of confidence needs to be maintained between the specialist and the student. Otherwise students will not feel free to come to the specialist with the very problems which need his attention. Such relationships as these obviously require a professionalized attitude toward the counseling work. But the main point is that the work of the specialized counselors needs to be tied in with the general program. The college physician, for example, needs also to be an educator in the sense of bringing his specialized knowledge of the student to bear on the student's all-round growth.

It is obvious from the foregoing analysis that the counseling program must be organized and integrated by a major administrative officer. This person needs a natural flair for the work, and also substantial training in personnel administration. He should have a genuine interest in the academic program and a vital connection with it. He should have an adequate measure of authority with the faculty, evidenced by an appropriate rank and title.

The counseling of students, then—using the term in the broad sense—is a function that lies at the heart of the educational program. It is not something extra, tacked onto the main academic job in order to care for peripheral matters or to check up on failures. It is an educational job because it starts where education must start—with the individual student. For it is through the counselor that the individual is stimulated, advised, and instructed, intellectually and otherwise, concerning the whole of his personal development.

The aim of counseling is to educate. In the educational process, it is necessary to start with the student where he is. Any other proposal risks failure. This means placing the student at the right level of achievement in subjects involving sequential skills; it means, equally, working with his social adjustment in the light of the habits, social and anti-social, he has acquired and the judgment he has achieved in his previous environment.

Consistent with starting to educate the individual where he is is the use of problems as educational opportunities. Awareness of a problem that is important to the individual is the nearest way to interest him in working toward a solution. These problems may be personal or social. The personal problems, to the extent that they affect the advancement of the student, need solution. But the counseling program should also be a primary medium through which students can be got interested in broader social problems. And interest leads directly to motivation.

Furthermore, the interest of the student is the key to stimulating and directing his thinking. Since development of the ability to think effectively is a first objective, it is essential to use the proper teaching technique. This is the technique of inducing the individual to think through the problem for himself, a method requiring both patience and skill. It does not preclude suggestions or instruction on the part of the teacher, but it does mean that the teacher must not impose his will or his views or conclusions on the student. The student should arrive at conclusions or decisions which are valid to him on the basis of his own reasoning. The instructor's job is to reason with him about his reasoning—that is, check and supplement his facts, criticize his hypotheses, suggest possible alternatives, and disprove the false or confirm the correct deductions. It is this kind of counseling which both stimulates critical inquiry and gains experience for the student in disciplined thinking. It is in this way that matured and discriminating judgment grows.

CHAPTER VI

INTELLECTUAL COMPETENCE

A MAN need not go through college in order to become educated. Many "self-made" men possess superior knowledge of present and past cultures or more effectiveness in applying thought to action than do many college graduates. Irrespective of whether they have been to college, the most genuinely educated men are those who take adequately broad views of their lifework. But college should be a period for the systematic and progressive accumulation of knowledge, for perfecting the ability to think, and for learning how to apply that thinking toward the advancement of contemporary culture. The program is therefore planned, and needs to be planned carefully, toward this end.

If the function of liberal education is to aid society to progress toward a higher level of culture, then the student must gain intellectual discrimination by examining facts, weighing values, and making judgments of the results, and must orient his emotional commitment to helping advance human progress. The task of the curriculum is to aid the individual in acquiring an understanding of, and competence in working with, both the broader problems of society and the special problems of the particular field to which he chooses to devote his major energies. He should gain a philosophical conception of his social culture as a whole, and at the same time a preparation for specific work in improving the culture.

The curriculum is an organized means through which the student can take advantage of the stimulation, counseling, and instruction which the teaching staff is able to offer. Organization implies opportunity—content, place, methods —for defining and enlarging upon the observations and problems of experience, assembling additional facts and noting the problems of other human experience, considering expert opinion and arguments of other explorers for wisdom, subjecting the data and ideas to analysis, and checking and verifying judgments formed and results obtained. The organized means include such interlocking devices as lectures, discussions, conferences, clinics, laboratory explorations, and theses. These methods are sufficiently familiar to need no exhaustive description or explanation here. Their statement in these terms, however, suggests a broad approach to the function of the classroom. They will be analyzed only enough to offer some suggestions for their improvement.

This definition of the function of liberal education implies a specific approach to determining what the curriculum should contain. The fundamental distinction between this approach and that commonly used is that it starts not with the idea of transmitting the cultural heritage of the past, but rather with the idea of applying man's intelligence toward the improvement of our present culture. The new approach, however, does not require a radical departure from the usual curriculum, but rather gives that curriculum a different focus or orientation.

This orientation is to the vital problems of society, both broadly general and specific. The production of synthetic materials to supplement natural resources, the better planning of our economic life, the designing of social organization on the international scale, and the total education of young people toward the good way of life are illustrations of these broad problems. The more specific problems arise in every field of human endeavor: disease control, conservation of natural resources, industrial strife, wealth and poverty, taxation, flood control, architectural design, how to lay out an efficient factory, education by radio and the motion picture, diet, the emotional adjustment of individuals, and so on. There is no dividing line between the general and the specific; they merge into each other. The specific grow out of the general, and the general must often be attacked through the specific fields. They all have something to do with a liberal education if they touch on what a contemporary scientist, Edwin G. Conklin, calls "the greatest problems that confront the human race," which he further defines as "how to promote social co-operation, how to increase loyalty to truth, how to promote justice, and a spirit of brotherhood; how to expand ethics until it embraces all mankind. These are problems for science as well as for government, education, and religion."[1]

No one person, and especially no student during four to six years of college, can hope to become competent to deal with any and all social problems. With the intense specialization that is essential in any field of endeavor today, the individual must gain competence in some particular field.

[1] Edwin Grant Conklin, "Science and Ethics," *Science*, Vol. 86, No. 2244, (December 31, 1937) p. 601.

But specialization alone is not enough. The whole is greater than the sum of the special fields. The group of specialists working together do not solve the whole of the problem: there is needed an over-all view of society, a view of its interrelationships, its perspective in time, and its trends and possibilities for the future. It does not suffice to say that there must be generalists as well as specialists. Men need to be both.

Curricula should not provide merely a judicious mixture of the "cultural" and the "special" subject matter. They should be dynamic, designed to help the individual obtain an adequate understanding of, and ability to work with, the culture in which he lives, as it applies both to life as a whole and to the field through which he is preparing to function. This principle extends as well to planning individual courses of study. For example, a well-planned course in mechanical engineering or in accounting should show the student the relevance of all that he learns both to his personal development and to social progress. Likewise, a course in philosophy should aid the student in determining his own basic objectives, including his vocational goal in life.

Culture is not a veneer to be got by studying either the introductory courses of the several fields of knowledge or the classics; it is a way of life. It implies effective living for social ends. It is not something in addition to, or on top of, the individual's field of work. It should be the essential motivating and governing force in that field, as well as in all other activities of the individual. From this it is evident that the curriculum should be planned around problems and materials which tend to bring together the general and the special, the cultural and the vocational, the theoretical and the practical.

Incidentally, it is because this integration is important that we may regret the way in which the inflexibility of the old arts curriculum forced the creation of numerous new schools, most of which went to the extreme in providing specialized and applied subject matter. They created a new rigidity of curriculum, as, for instance, in the engineering school; fortunately, a move to correct this tendency is now evident. Many teachers' colleges, for example, have been converted into "state colleges" with an accompanying enrichment of the curriculum. The test is not that of "either-or"— or even of "both"—general and field, cultural and vocational, or theoretical and practical. Rather it is the way they blend and become a unity in the life and work of the individual. For a particular curriculum, the question becomes one of proportion and of relative emphasis. But generally speaking, it is to the best interest of society that all individuals intelligent enough to profit by higher education should have a curriculum which both emphasizes the more significant general problems of society and at the same time aids the individual in obtaining some proficiency in creative work in specialized fields. Or, to put it another way, liberal education needs to be an active ingredient in all curricula of higher education.

A survey of students' intellectual interests will readily show that they are conditioned by the typical problems which have grown out of their own environment, and which are largely those of society in general. There is sufficient common ground here to serve as a point of departure. With all students studying these broad, general problems, the field interests can grow out of the more specialized consideration of some of them. In the end, the field exists primarily because it contributes to the whole. There is inherent in this approach a method of reconciling the special interests of the student with society's broader needs.

It is proposed, then, that the curriculum in liberal education should be focused around the study of the vital problems in society. The specific arrangement of these general problems in the curriculum can vary greatly; experimentation must find the best method. Roughly, the problems can be selected for their timeliness—international organization, for example, has become of paramount interest through the outbreak of another general war; or they can be arranged by their simplicity or complexity, their local bearing or larger significance. Possibly a combination of the two methods would be desirable, allowing students to study a broader problem at the same time they are studying a number of lesser ones also. Criteria for the selection of particular problems might be their importance to society and their educational value as determined by a consensus of the college group. More specific criteria might be the light they shed on the general culture of society, their relationship to the present and the past, and their usefulness in coupling thought to action in the present and the future. Enough problems exist, certainly, to more than fill several curricula.

After the problems have been selected, the work needs to be carefully planned in order to bring out all of the significant ramifications, both in relationships and in time. In the study of power, for example, there is, broadly, the creation of power, its utilization, and the control over it. There are the different forms of power upon which successive civilizations have been built—the domestication of animals, human slavery, water, coal, gas and oil, electricity. And we begin to speculate upon the possibility of creating new power through photosynthesis, utilizing the sun as the source of energy. Changes like these revolutionize life. The same problem may be defined more specifically in terms of particular relationships, such as relief from human routine and drudgery, provision of more abundant supplies of the necessities and conveniences of life, use for either the improvement or the destruction of civilization; and again, power may be considered in even more specific terms, such as engineering design, governmental regulation or control, the conservation of natural resources, or the ethics of particular uses of power. One or two or more such broad problems might be studied each year.

Or if the approach from the more elementary to the complex is preferred, the problems can be arranged by years on this basis: At the start, some of the more localized and practical problems, such as housing, relief administration, community health, and local politics and government could be chosen. During the second year, the broader problems involved in, say, industrial production, agriculture, engineering, and disease control might be studied. For a third year, the more intangible problems arising from habits and customs, morals, individual and group psychologies, industrial organization, and regional planning would be available. And finally in the larger realm of philosophy, the problems of economic planning, population control, the provision of educational opportunities, and world-order planning might be drawn upon. These are mentioned as random, not specific, suggestions.

For such an approach, the available sources of materials are many. Perhaps it should be said parenthetically here that there are always difficulties in shifting from one type of curriculum to another. Probably it is easier to shift the whole curriculum to a new basis than to shift a single course, but lack of materials and experience with a new method are genuine handicaps. Where the single instructor adapts his course to the new approach, he may have to compromise at the start by using illustrative problems found in the standard textbooks. Otherwise, because most problems are comprehensive, the treatment may be superficial. Added to the usual sources of books, motion pictures, and the lectures of instructors are—if the full program suggested herein is used —the personal observations and experiences of the student in the campus activities and his off-campus explorations and work. The tie-in between the various phases of the program is apparent.

Generally speaking, every educational device—lectures, motion pictures, discussion meetings, laboratory exercises, and conferences—would be utilized. An advantage of constructing this portion of the curriculum in larger blocs than single courses is that it allows a much more flexible method. In part, for instance, the work can be handled in large groups, as where lectures for orientation or of interpretation are given. On the other hand, the work can be highly individualized through the individual studies and special theses or reports prepared by the students. A series of major theses, presented at regular intervals throughout the years at college, would have distinct educational value. They are an excellent medium through which to develop clarity of thinking and of expression (through which to teach English composition with more fruitful results, perhaps, than flow from the usual composition course) and to make the learning process genuine. Their preparation necessitates thorough and accurate work; and the knowledge acquired from selecting and analyzing materials has to be digested and made a part of the student's working equipment. They are also a good device through which the counselor can participate in the instruction of the student. Properly handled, the study of these major problems can lead to competence in several directions.

To direct the study of the broad problems that cut across several of the usual fields of more intensive study, there should be a specific administrative setup. An advantage of this organization of the curriculum is that here at least a portion of it gets unified direction from the faculty. It would no longer be possible for departmental heads to maintain jurisdiction over particular segments of the general program, as they do when the general curriculum consists of the introductory courses from each of several departments. One step in this direction, which would also direct the student in his work, is the preparation of careful syllabi. The syllabus is a plan of action. It analyzes the objectives to be sought; outlines the attack; presents essential materials not available otherwise; suggests further exploration or experimentation by the student in laboratory, readings, and references; indicates how the instruction will be given; and states the standards of, and methods of measuring, achievement.

It does not contradict what has been said here if some specific courses have to be carried parallel with this work. Students with weak high-school training in grammar or mathematics, for instance, may need special clinic courses.

Many will have had inadequate laboratory training or not know how to use the library; and special instruction will have to be arranged. To acquire proficiency in the use of a foreign language, also, students have to take specific courses of study. Also, a general reading program is needed, which will both supplement and complement the study of social problems. But since it has additional objectives, it will be discussed in the following chapter.

The criticisms of the typical "survey" or "general cultural" courses in the present-day curriculum attack the *content* of the courses, not the *use* of courses as a curriculum structural device. However, as already noted, there is merit in centering this phase of the curriculum around broad theses, based upon syllabi, scheduled according to the individual's progress in his particular field and to his extracurricular and extramural experiences. The use of the thesis method, and of the general reading program suggested in Chapter VII, obviously would require a considerable change in, and extension of, the counseling and tutorial functions of teachers.

The study of the broader social problems should be continued each year throughout the college course. This contrasts with the common practice of confining "general education" to the first two years of college. As the student approaches the responsibilities of citizenship and of civic leadership, he should be broadening his social orientation. But this study need not occupy more than its appropriate share of the student's time, a considerable part of which should be devoted to securing competence in a special field. Such special fields include, of course, those already common to the liberal arts colleges—English, economics, chemistry, biology, and so forth—although the fields should not be limited either to these usual ones or to fields as they are defined by the usual departmental organization.

Right here an important distinction should be drawn between the departmental or divisional organization of the college and the field of concentration for the student. Both have their functions. The former is an administrative necessity: in the selection of faculty, the designing of departmental courses of study, the ordering and handling of books and laboratory supplies, and the searching for desirable supplementary experiences for students, on campus and off. The field of concentration, however, need not be synonymous with the department of the college, although for some students it may be so incidentally. The *field* should be an area of major or specialized study for the student. It is an arrangement of courses personal with him and meeting his needs. For the student, his field should start with the more specific problems in which he becomes interested, and should draw upon courses from any or all departments of the college. The pattern to be followed is not a preconceived structure of subject matter, but rather a sequence and arrangement of courses of study that will best contribute to the individual's whole development and to the special studies he desires to undertake.

The choice of these courses should be directed but not dictated by the college. Such criteria as their homogeneity, or progression in intensity of study, or the general or rounded view they give of a particular area of knowledge should be set up. These criteria should then be used by the counselor in guiding the student in his selection of specific courses. It is reasonable to ask the student to plan the layout beforehand, and to defend the plan on the basis of his own reasoning; but there are advantages in not dictating to him the specific courses he must take. His counselor should likewise be of his own selection, although it is reasonable to insist on college approval of the choice on the basis of the instructor's preparation in the general area of the student's field. The point is that the counselor should not automatically be the head of the department most nearly resembling the field chosen. The counselor, in turn, should be under the direction of the central counseling officer of the college.

Incidentally, making an effective distinction between department and field has an important bearing upon the quality of the college curriculum. Changes like these are directed at making the organization of the college more nearly functional. That is, placing the general curriculum and the work in counseling under central administrative officers, and removing these responsibilities from department heads, secures for both general curriculum and counseling the unified direction of competent leaders who can give them the interest and the careful attention they deserve. Relieving the departments of their authority over the students frees the students to make selections among courses on the basis of personal interest and course merit. The enticing of students to become majors in order to swell enrollments, and thus to get more finances for the department, is reduced. Badly taught, superficial, and ineffective courses are dropped, because enrollment in these courses can no longer be required. The opinion of students and counselors concerning the teaching effectiveness of instructors is made more evident, and poor instructors can be assisted to improve their work or be eliminated. Where administrative consolidations seem advisable, the way is open. Course consolidations, in particular, become possible, reducing duplications and overlappings. New courses have a better chance to be judged on their merit rather than on the basis of politics.

The adoption of this proposal will bring pressure upon the institution to add new departments from which course selections may be made for the fields. To the extent that this pressure opens up fields of opportunity, it is an excellent thing. The colleges have been inclined only grudgingly to move away from the traditional departments. Educational theory and practice has joined the curricular family, after a considerable struggle, in most liberal arts colleges; business, engineering, and the applied arts in some places have acquired footholds. Naturally, it is not desirable for the college to open new departments merely for the sake of presenting long lists of "new" courses—something which commonly happens in education and engineering, for example. But neither is it advisable to exclude new departments when it can be demonstrated on merit that the prospective additions are basic and important. In solving this enigma, we have to consider what the new courses are. For the most part they tend to be new orientations of materials old in themselves, or applications of old materials.

The task in curriculum construction, then, lies in determining the basic fields, and limiting the course offerings to them. The structure of departmental courses can stand much as it is today, and with good reason. The fields already use, substantially, the contemporary-problem approach in building their courses. Ordinarily, they do not start with something considered to be "good" for the student, but rather set out to give him a measure of competence in dealing with the problems of the field. Preparation in a field inherently assumes a thorough grounding in its principles and methods, which in turn necessitates certain course sequences. A chemist, for example, must be a capable chemist, aware of the problems of chemistry and able to define and analyze them. He progresses from a study of basic principles to qualitative and quantitative analysis, and from there into organic or into physical chemistry. In most fields in the arts and sciences today, genuine competence necessitates graduate study also.

But, on the other hand, the students should be permitted great flexibility in choosing from the various departmental offerings. The student then makes his own applications. For example, there need be no "Department of Public Administration" for the student to major in public administration. He can construct an essentially sound major by making selections from economics, political science, psychology, sociology, and engineering. Logically, the student of engineering should become a more creative engineer if his courses include a liberal allotment of the basic sciences rather than purely engineering courses. Journalism is a legitimate field of work— one of social value and significance. But specialized courses training for journalism are less valuable than courses in creative writing, literature, psychology, sociology, history, and economics. Especially is this true if there is provision for off-campus newspaper or journalistic work. Combinations of these courses, rather than a major either in a Department of Journalism or the English Department, make the best preparation for one's lifework in the field.

In fact, in the light of the possible combinations which can be made, a curriculum even smaller than that of the average college would become greatly richer in its possibilities for the individual if students were not forced to major in a "department" of the college. The plan assumes, of course, skillful and informed direction on the part of the counselors.

Important in this process of change in the curriculum is the test of quality rather than quantity. The attempt of an instructor who is steeped in his particular field to present *all* of his knowledge to his students defeats the very aim of education. Enthusiasm for a subject is essential, but if the subject is overpresented, the main objective may be lost—to teach the student how to think in the field. Furthermore, it is desirable not thus to exhaust knowledge by exposing it all at once; the student ought to be left with some incentive to keep studying! The teacher should whet the student's appetite—not overstuff him. The college faculty may therefore safely leave gaps in the curriculum, and confine their efforts to the areas of greatest importance and to those in which they may undertake a high quality of work.

In the fields of concentration, the necessity for continuing much the same courses of study as the colleges now give is tacitly assumed. There should, however, be two qualifications to this assumption. The first is that the tendency to emphasize departments more and more, and to devote less time to a comprehensive study of problems and materials, leads to a narrow vocationalism in liberal education—a vocationalism which the colleges hide, even from themselves, by shouting their opposition to vocational education. The methods suggested should tend to reduce this departmentalization of knowledge. The second qualification is that there should be adequate provision for individualized work. If in a student's study of broad social problems, especially near the start of the field work, his interest lights on some special problem, he should be given the opportunity under the guidance of his counselor to make an intensive study of it. Likewise, in his more advanced years, if his plan of study suggests the need for an individualized application of the theory he has been studying, he should be encouraged to work out a syllabus and the resulting thesis or report should be considered part of his field achievement. Or if he wants to pursue the subject matter of a course beyond the requirements of the syllabus, he should be permitted to do so and receive appropriate time-allowance in his program. The advantages seem obvious.

To summarize briefly: If the design of the curriculum were based upon the vital problems of society, the study of the more comprehensive ones would orient the student to the culture in which he lives, and the more intensive study of those in a particular field would give him a preparation for his life work. The two phases of the study thus have a common approach. The apparent incompatibility of general education and of field specialization is resolved. And the whole of the curriculum relates functionally to the needs of society.

CHAPTER VII

THE SEARCH FOR HIGHER VALUES

EVENTS of the past century have had a disintegrating effect upon liberal education. There was the impact of new theories in science—in particular Darwin's theory of evolution—which, on the one hand, controverted orthodox religion and, on the other, opened up vast areas for the search of new knowledge. There was the Marxian theory of history and of economics, which gradually undermined the entrenched classical doctrines. There was the Freudian theory of human behavior, which broke new ground in this field. There was the impact of the advanced stages of the Industrial Revolution, whose leaders and workmen hungered for new techniques; and which also brought inventions in communication which allowed us to tap quickly the knowledge available in contemporary cultures other than our own.

There were three results of these impacts: the undermining of the dogmas upon which the religious approach to education had depended; a gradual displacement of laissez-faire attitudes toward economic life by the notion that more rapid and equitable progress can be made through planning economic activity; and a tremendous stimulation to new learning on the frontiers of knowledge. A natural result was a great spontaneous development in the material well-being of the world, which had the effect of blinding us to its disintegrating influence upon education. The process was partly one of division. Each branch of human knowledge divided, and in turn subdivided, many times.

Increase in knowledge was good; but accompanying this increase was the destruction of the "absolutes" of the past. The church was so tied to its creeds that it was unable to adjust rapidly to the new ideas. Hence it was always lagging behind in its interpretation of the meaning of life in the face of new facts. Thus it lost its influence with the educated group, with the intellectual leaders. This was destructive to liberal education, because it was the church that up to this point had given the colleges their stimulation and ethical direction. In fact, the Christian dogma was the framework on which the whole body of knowledge was built up.

Within the college, the craving for the new knowledge resulted in a rapidly expanding curriculum—new departments and new schools—always in the direction of specialization. The little body of literature about Western culture, and the mathematics and languages supposed to "sharpen the mind" for use in any discipline, were gradually displaced in favor of specialized courses, largely emphasizing techniques. What had been the content of liberal education became squeezed into superficial survey courses in the first two years of college in order to make room for the new growth in the curriculum.

This happened not only within the four-year college. The law curriculum, for example, which formerly had been a treatise on human behavior and social organization, became an intensified case study of techniques in winning legal disputes. The newer curricula in the schools of education, engineering, business administration, and so forth were devoted to techniques, and seldom undertook an analysis of over-all purposes.

The compulsion with the student was to learn skills and thereby become successful in this new material world which was unfolding with such dazzling and seemingly inexhaustible vigor. The compulsion on the professor was to isolate new facts—in science, in social science, in history—and his academic career depended upon the fruitfulness of his search at the periphery of knowledge. Thus he became "objective," a fact finder. As he discovered new facts he became a debunker. He became cautious in dealing with knowledge and timid in making judgments about its meaning. He became cynical. For him the word "moral" was outmoded; it was not smart to be "moralistic."

The new pragmatic philosophy was a contributing factor to this end result. It was a good philosophy; it was a necessary substitute for the absolutes which had been discarded. It promoted the experimental attitude toward learning and toward life. But pragmatism also had one effect that was bad. The typical college professor, become a devotee of pragmatism without understanding its true import—the use of hypotheses to be tested by experience—became unwilling to make judgments until after history had turned the corner. Because human destiny (for the intellectual) was no longer determined by the will of God, life became more or less automatic, with the interpretations of meaning being made as post-mortems.

Probably most in default have been the historians, who, along with the writers, should be the special guardians of the humanities. In their search for new facts, they turned to a piecemeal analysis of small segments of human activity, uncovering a wealth of new information, but failing to interpret these facts in terms of giving to civilization direction for the future. Like the scientist, they were fact finders; they defaulted at the point where their facts became significant, in their fundamental role as philosophers.

Liberal education, then, has come to a crossroads. The form and direction it received from religion is for the most part gone, its traditional four-year content has been so adulterated as to be no longer recognizable, and its service in making value judgments on human progress has largely been lost. On the other hand, the proponents of liberal education have been slow to recognize the new function which liberal education should have in the world today.

We are in a complex stage of civilization, where a more comprehensive view of the possibilities for life on earth is needed. We are catching glimpses of these possibilities as we profit by the explorations that have followed the work of Darwin, Marx, Freud and others. For example, our imaginations respecting the natural development of life have been completely reoriented by understanding how living matter progressed through the geologic ages. Now thinking men are beginning to speculate upon the possibilities that may lie in applying the scientific method to social organization. Already enough "five-year plans" have been tried to give some evidence of the results which can flow through social planning. And the present war forcefully illustrates the chaos that results from the failure to solve the large social problems through the orderly processes of group thinking. The frame of reference of this life planning is a faith in human beings, all human beings, and their ability to use their intelligence to achieve a fuller life and a higher social culture. This is the basic premise of democracy as a way of life.

Planning assumes an ability to appraise values, to judge what is most worth pursuing, what is social and what antisocial. It assumes a sense of direction and a will to improve. It assumes, on the part of the students, a growing philosophy of life. The search for higher values requires both intellectual discrimination (to know them) and emotional drive (to achieve them).

In earlier chapters such terms as "improve," "higher," and "finer" have repeatedly been used. These words and phrases are, of course, relative. They can denote different standards in different times, under varying circumstances, or as applied to various things. The solutions to problems, too, are relative. What appears to be solved satisfactorily today may tomorrow prove to be unsolved. Problems are but points of attack, approaches toward improvement; they ordinarily represent those points of strain in human relationships which most obviously need adjustment. The human problem as a whole is never "solved," for improvement in one direction merely puts other factors out of line and creates new problems. Progress in life may be likened to William James's description of the stream of consciousness in that it resembles "an alternation of flights and perchings." [1] In a revolutionary period such as the present, the flights create much hardship because they are exaggerated, but we must remember that in a complex civilization there is inevitably an increase in the variety of problems to be solved.

The approach to higher values in civilization is of necessity

[1] William James, *The Principles of Psychology*, Vol. 1, p. 243. New York: Henry Holt and Company, 1890.

experimental. Society, like individuals, must make successive trials and evaluations to reach the higher levels of culture. If we assume the continuously more adequate use of our intelligence, there is no valid reason for the repetition of human experience which has proved unfruitful or bad. Individual experience builds up the intuitional reactions of the individual so that he avoids the repetition of costly errors; but social experience, more complex, is a reliable guide only as intelligent men dissect and analyze this experience and attempt to apply its lessons to the present.

We have not as yet learned how to do this well. We Americans are still so flushed with the success of our laissez-faire method that we have not stopped to analyze why it succeeded so well for a time, and why it has begun to fail so badly now. Of course, that statement is not quite true. Two successive presidents, Herbert Hoover and Franklin D. Roosevelt, have each in turn had prepared comprehensive studies of the social trends in America—but the studies have been largely ignored. Periodical evaluation and planning of national policy will, presently, become the accepted procedure. It will come because we are too intelligent to accept the alternative, chaos.

How inadequate and how provincial our American culture suddenly appears in the light of the two major crises which have recently occurred—the depression of the thirties and the second World War! Incongruously offsetting the high standard of living, which is our pride and the envy of the world, are the terrible blemishes in our social fabric which have been exposed by the depression—poverty, neglected disease, slums, barriers to higher education, racial conflicts, wasted soil and natural resources, thwarted opportunity for a substantial portion of the population. Confronting us are some major issues of which we are so far only dimly aware— for example, the effects of our drifting national eugenics policy. Confronting us, too, is the bald fact that as yet we have made little contribution, beyond the materialistic one, to human advancement. At least, we have little to show in the fields men have deemed most cultural—in literature, in art, in music, in religion, and in philosophy.

How provincial in outlook and knowledge we suddenly seem when the war forces us to look at ourselves from a world perspective! Our exclusive devotion to the classics of the Western world has left us without an understanding of the East; yet the Orient has a culture much older than ours, and one which is again rapidly becoming influential. Will our future relationships between West and East be based upon mutual understanding and respect, or upon the distrust and suspicion born of ignorance? We have centered our attention upon the Jewish-Christian religion, disregarding the spiritual heritages which shape the thoughts and emotions of more than half the world's population. Will we not have to explore for common ground among these religions in order to develop the tolerance that promotes world unity? Our dogmatic belief in a particular way to organize economic society has left us intolerant of suggestions for improvement; yet we discover that Germany and Japan have been able to prosecute prolonged wars without having "adequate" gold reserves, and that Russia in the brief space of twenty years has by an unorthodox economy transformed herself from peasant status to a powerful, industrialized nation.

If men could just look down on their handiwork from on high, how ridiculous would seem the repeated struggles for power between the Anglo-Saxons and the Germans, the attitude of superiority which the white race has developed toward those with darker skin pigments, the prejudices which exist between Christians and Jews, the slums which surround prosperous factories, the dirt, disease, and malnutrition which exist in spite of the health and sanitary knowledge we possess! Would these celestial observers be able to describe the values by which we work?

Descending from these speculations to the subject at hand, we must admit that our American educational process falls short of what it might be. For our provincialism and our weaknesses are in good part due to the narrow vision which the confined study of our own cultural heritage has given us. The process of having our children acquire a liberal education has been analogous to that of having them learn as apprentices the family skills or trades—they have learned only what the particular family has learned through earlier experience. This limited study has had, and continues to have, value; but it is time to extend our horizons.

We need to search all other human experience if we are to find the best values known to men. This embraces our own culture and all others. It includes an examination of the culture of today, and of its development from the past.

The attainment of excellence is an evolving process with its roots in the past, its effort in the present, and its direction set tentatively for the future. If our immediate experience is to be better, we must know what other men, present and past, have considered good. We must appraise the merit of their ideas in the light of experience. And we must, further, project ideas of our own, and through trial and error attempt to move ahead.

Knowledge of the past and of other contemporary cultures is especially valuable as perspective for the present. Any inventor knows that his work is not the inspiration of a moment. The radio, for instance, is not simply a set of ingenious mechanical parts recently "dreamed up" in the laboratory. It is one fruit of men's intellectual growth—in mathematics, physics, electronics—over several centuries of time. Or, to use another example, no opinion on the causes of the fluctuating business cycle is valid unless it is based in part upon a knowledge of the cyclical movements since the beginning of the Industrial Revolution. Or to put it still another way, a comparison of the church painters of earlier generations with the modern muralists discloses a common zeal to stir men toward higher ideals. Charles Dickens' description of American manners and customs of a century ago gives us a partial basis for evaluating those of today.

We need especially to gain perspective on ideas. Compare, for instance, the views of successive generations concerning the place of women in society. Look back now upon the temerity with which women were admitted to higher education for the first time just a century ago! Or as another illustration, consider how perfectly expressed, after nearly six hundred years of formulation, the civil liberties of our Constitution were thought to be—until a changed economic era brought demands for the recognition of new rights. Or again, it is useful to compare the philosophical serenity of the Chinese, and the devotion to peace of the East Indians, with the aggressive characteristics of Western people, and to attempt to account for and to evaluate these differences in philosophy. Important, too, is an understanding of the utopias and the moral and ethical codes devised in the past, and of the way ideas like these can stimulate the imagination and thinking of the leaders of the present.

Men's ideas of what constitutes perfection need tempering and revision in the light of experience. Painters of the seventeenth century had seemingly made "perfect" matchings of color—as perfectly matched as the human eye could determine; but the modern spectrophotometer makes possible still greater perfection. Philosophers have long speculated upon what constitutes "perfect" human behavior. They have said that temperance, honesty, justice do. But these are abstractions which become real only through action. And the Chinese conception of honesty, or the Frenchman's notion of temperance, or the Russian's idea of justice may differ from our own. Possibly we are "right" in our ideas of perfection, but the intelligent man should not be too sure of his convictions until he has appraised other human experience.

Sensitivity to relative values depends in part upon how far the individual has shared experience wider than his own—in particular, as far as he can, has shared the motives and sensations of those who have created things of lasting value. The sensitivity is quickened if the individual makes some attempt to re-create the artist's work. Taking part in a play, for instance, enables the individual to understand much better the methods and ends of the drama. And the study of, and participation in, fine music develops the emotional responses in the direction of genuine quality.

Closely related to discriminating judgment of, and sensitivity to, values is the gaining of intellectual and emotional inspiration. This comes from many sources, and differs greatly among individuals; but a primary source lies in living with and enjoying the treasures and discoveries which have accumulated from the past. They are too varied to try to suggest —a trilobite for one person, a finely cut diamond for another, or a glimpse of Jupiter through a telescope for a third may be the thing which fires the imagination. But obviously the more enduring treasures are most available among the arts, music, literature, scientific specimens, and the observable folkways of people.

The continuity in the flow of thinking through the generations is what permits these appraisals of values to be made. Our ability to communicate fully with one another is dependent upon our ability to verbalize the accumulated experiences of the past—and upon this slender thread depends the whole of our complex civilization. And in so far as intellectual and emotional inspiration and commitment come from these ideas and past achievements, there is gained for society the will on the part of individuals to fight for still higher ideals and greater achievements.

This analysis can be summarized in educational terms by saying that sensitivity to certain individual and social values comes through a study of men's past ideas and experiences, and of other racial or national cultures contemporary with our own. This gives the individual a "better"—i.e., more discriminating—basis for selecting his active interests. These interests lead to greater emotional enjoyment of living and to the more creative use of time—both important in realizing the fullest personal development. The individual, too, gains perspective on human affairs, and can thus face crises more objectively and in consequence utilize his intelligence to better advantage for society and with greater satisfaction to himself. With this perspective comes a certain freedom from fear, superstition, and distrust. Knowledge and appreciation of the finer achievements of the human mind, and more gracious ways of living, also assist the individual in enjoying finer human relationships, and in improving his immediate environment.

The strength of the individual is automatically infused into society. Hence, individual values carry over into social advantages. The greater the perspective with which persons regard social problems, for instance, the more likely they are to determine upon preferable courses of action. When goals are considered in terms of the whole of human progress, the inevitable adjustments in human relationships and in the choice of further goals can more easily be made.

Granted the desirability of seeking, in college, values like these, how can the college program be implemented to secure them? In general, the important thing is to see that the curriculum is thoroughly informed with the point of view and enriched with the content suggested. There are many ways of accomplishing this; however, the program as already outlined is largely capable of satisfying the purpose. Four provisions in particular bear on the problem: the drawing upon past and present cultures in studying the vital problems of society; the inclusion of a wide background of human knowledge in the course offerings in the various fields of concentration; the encouragement of the active arts, including the fine arts, not only curricularly but in extraclass activities as well; and the opportunity which the field experience, discussed in a later chapter, offers in getting acquainted with the life, work, and cultural facilities of the various communities in which the students work or which they visit.

This experience is an important phase of the search for higher values, because cultural wisdom is not a distilled "something" that can be handed to, or lectured at, the student. Wisdom is an application of knowledge to present action, and therefore must rest upon a foundation of experience in the life of the student himself. This means that the student's opportunities to observe his contemporary culture must be greatly enlarged in order that his study of the past and of other cultures can have meaning in terms of the present. The heart of this educational process is that interaction between the individual's own experience and his growing understanding of the accumulated experience of men on earth. That is the efficient way to learn. Man is distinguished from other forms of life in that he can use his intelligence to profit by the experience of those who have gone before or who live in remote lands. It is this that enables him to plan his life and his society.

The end product we are seeking in college, however, is the alumnus who will undertake in life a role of the kind we have been discussing. The provisions of the college program outlined above correspond roughly to the major activities of the socially minded and intellectually active college graduate. That is, he will devote time to the problems of his society, he will work actively in some vocational or professional field, and he will join in the cultural and civic life of his community. The suggested program is designed to give the student a laboratory training in living in order to provide the maximum influence in postcollege life.

In this scheme there is one weak link. In college a student has the continuous direction of his teachers. They help him to interpret his experiences and to plan further programs for himself; and the courses of study provide a steady source of new inspiration. After college, the alumnus is on his own.

What is it that continues to aid him in his search for knowledge and for values? Probably many things help do this, but the most obvious one is his own reading program. Reading is the main artery through which the individual receives a transfusion of ideas.

Now one aim of the liberal college is to induce lifetime habits of reading literature of quality and significance. But it is well-known that, on the average, the college graduate quickly slips back into the habit of reading what drops into his lap from the daily paper or second-class mail delivery—if that. The thread of cultural stimulation becomes a fragile one.

At least part of this failure of the college education to take root in the individual's life lies in the way college reading is done. Several criticisms seem pertinent: the reading is chopped up into small courses, with no sustained continuity or theme running throughout; these courses are taken by the student chiefly to accumulate grades and credits, so that his basic incentive in the work is a false one; and once he has passed the courses, he quickly forgets them. Furthermore, the reading tends to be extensive rather than intensive, with little meaning to the student; or, again, in some courses it will undergo a minute dissection which may be of technical merit but will hardly conduce to giving the student an appetite for reading. Finally, it is common practice in the colleges to restrict the reading of the students to secondary sources—the bulk of it to textbooks, which are often dull. These policies seem shortsighted, emphasizing, as they do, certain immediate and specific results rather than the larger result of cultivating lifetime interests and habits.

It is unfortunate that the average college program makes

no provision for cultural reading of the kind the college hopes its graduates will do later. Aside from the few colleges which permit the better students to do autonomous, "honors," or "tutorial" work, there is no such provision in the typical curriculum, no incentive or time for the average student to do reading on his own. The requisites for such a reading program would seem to be: sufficient continuity and time to help make the reading habitual; enough choice to allow it to be coupled with active interests of the individual, and to permit intensive reading in fields of special interest; sufficient planning on the part both of the college and of the student to have the reading work toward a sense of values; and adequate preparation on the part of the counselor to enable him not only to stimulate the interest and guide the reading of the student but to discuss the subject matter with him. The kinds of values sought in this reading—intellectual discrimination and perspective, emotional stimulation and responsiveness, factual knowledge and intuitional judgment, intellectual appetite—are not realized overnight, nor in haphazardly related or superficial courses. They require continuous and careful cultivation over several years of time. They also require that the materials read be analyzed in terms of the student's application of them to his own life. Indeed, a wise counselor will aid the student in interpreting his own personal problems through drawing upon this reading.

Within reasonable limits, the student may be expected to direct his reading to secure specific knowledge. A knowledge of the theory of evolution, or of the history of the democratic form of government, or of how matter and energy behave, or of the influence of the great religions of the world, or of a few outstanding works of fiction, to suggest a few examples, should be expected of the individual possessing a liberal education.

To summarize and particularize: Time should be allowed in the student's program during each of his years in college for general reading. This program should be planned between the student and his counselor to seek the objectives outlined above. Carefully prepared syllabi should state these objectives and offer liberal suggestions of topics, books, and procedures. If the students spend periods in work away from the campus, the reading should be continued through such periods. Indeed, these periods are especially opportune for reading on problems observed during the off-campus experience. Conferences for the evaluation of ideas should be held at regular intervals. (If the college cannot afford such individualized work, the reading program can be organized around group projects.) In a way, this reading program might be described as a running course in the philosophy of life, continuous in sequence throughout the college years— and, we may hope, afteryears.

The student's search for higher values can be further assisted by writing, under the direction of his counselor, an occasional "life aims" paper. This paper should be both intimate and comprehensive. It should digest the ideas accumulated by the student and synthesize them with his own life philosophy. If well done at perhaps three intervals—the beginning, halfway, and at graduation—during the college course, the papers should help to give the student an ethical direction for his life. Incidentally, if this self-appraisal under the guidance of the college were repeated a couple of times (say at five-year intervals) following graduation, it might stimulate the graduate toward further intellectual growth.

A final question relative to curriculum construction will be on the lips of every college administrator: What relative proportions of time should be devoted by the student to the three primary elements of the course of study—the study of broad social problems, the field of concentration, and the reading program? The answer might depend upon the individual's relative background, achievements, and needs. One student may as a freshman already have a sensitivity to fine quality, a second may have well-matured plans to do his specialized work in professional or graduate school, and a third may already be motivated and possess some competence for social action.

Aside from individualizing the program to fit needs, there is no reason for emphasizing one particular phase of the program at the expense of the others. Competence in a field is essential, but for most fields appropriate to the liberal arts college such competence cannot be wholly secured during the undergraduate period. The broad problems selected for study can be limited to the most vital or educationally beneficial ones; they are merely representative of the problems with which the individual will continue to work after college. It is more important that the student prepare one thesis carefully than that he dash off three superficially. Finally, the quality and interestingness of the general reading materials is more important than their quantity. The three phases of the program tend to blend together. The special field, the broader social problems, and the general reading are all designed to bring about growth in the student and should be well co-ordinated through having continuous reference to one another. The important tests for the student are his progress in total growth, the ethical direction he has acquired, and a continuing curiosity and search after values which ensures that he will continue his education for many years to come.

CHAPTER VIII

CRITICAL INQUIRY

WHATEVER else it may be, the college should above all be the place where intelligence and action go hand in hand. *Intelligence in action* means intellectual integrity and intellectual responsibility. The former means that the individual must use his intelligence in accord with his own best beliefs and purposes in life; the latter means that he must use intelligence for social, as distinguished from antisocial, ends.

Integrity and responsibility together imply the pursuit of truth—not for its own sake, but as the road to the best way of life. It follows that it is the privilege and the obligation of the intelligent man, in college, to search for knowledge that will aid in advancing along this road.

Truth-hunting has its negative as well as its positive side. Negatively, one must surmount the obstacles which hold back the expanding frontiers of knowledge—superstition, dogmatism, interfering special privileges, or blind spots due to personal bias. On the positive side, one must engage in systematic search for the truth, by the discovery and assembling of facts, and by applying to them the scientific method of analysis and synthesis.

It is again the privilege and the responsibility of the intelligent man to disclose to society the knowledge he has gained, when he has sufficiently tested its validity and when the knowledge seems of pertinent social significance. The individual's integrity and responsibility must be the deciding factors. But it is, of course, part of the educational institution's job to encourage the development of these two traits in individuals, along with the additional trait of discriminating judgment.

Social responsibility must be distinguished carefully from license. License—in the guise of unwarranted attacks upon others, or of knowingly imputing wrong motives to others, or of issuing facts carelessly framed or deliberately misinterpreted—implies the opposite of objectivity, of integrity, or of critical inquiry. It is as important in the intellectual sphere that license be reduced and eliminated as it is, say, in driving an automobile. The careless intellectual driver can do as much harm to individual and social freedom as the careless automobile driver can do to life and limb.

There is also a distinction between objectivity and indifference or neutrality. Objectivity does not mean that the individual must forever refrain from arriving at opinions of his own. True, he should be open-minded and be ready to change his beliefs as new evidence comes to light. But for full living, both individually and socially, individuals must possess convictions and be willing and able to act upon them. Nowhere is this more important than in college. The instructor who never voices an opinion, who weasels out of every situation, or who observes life but does not participate in its significant activities is hardly a suitable counselor and instructor for young people. It is unfortunate that social pressures sometimes tend to bring about this effect, but the value of the instructor to the students and to society is cut in half if his wisdom is not accompanied by courage. The distinction between expressing personal opinions and educating, however, must be clear. For educating is the process of aiding the student in arriving at opinions and judgments of his own. The instructor must therefore avoid pressing his opinions upon the student, or insisting upon their finality, because that defeats his own ends. The pursuit of knowledge is the task of a lifetime, and the student must be encouraged always to follow the inquiry further, and to meet all expressions of opinion with an attitude of critical inquiry.

The use of significant social problems—many of them highly controversial—as a basis for the general curriculum of the college necessitates encouraging and maintaining critical inquiry, and intellectual responsibility and integrity. The consideration of such problems, and the voicing of opinions about them, invariably brings upon the institution a varied assortment of social pressures and emotional situations which may threaten the institution's very life. Now, killing a college is the quickest way to defeat its whole purpose; as in war, a penetration too deep within the enemy lines may cause the salient to be cut off, and the main objective defeated. Thus, when advocating reforms which run counter to contemporary opinions and interests, one must use skill and strategy. In particular, within a group that develops a zeal for reform, rash or impetuous action based upon superficial observations and judgments needs to be restrained. Surrender or compromise is not necessarily the remedy, however. Exempting obvious social problems from inquiry within the college may bring a temporary gain—release from pressures or some reward such as increased financial security—but the practice strikes at the vitality of the institution. The

college, as well as the individual, must have the courage of
its convictions. It must do as well as it can the educational
job that is its function. And society, in the long run, has a
way of rewarding courage and vitality.

A moment's reflection will show the advantages to society
in permitting full and free discussion of, and critical inquiry
into, social problems. For one thing the youth of today meet
these problems in their everyday experiences. They are both
stimulated and confused by them. They discuss some of them
almost continuously. They no longer are molded in their
attitudes toward these issues, as the young people of former
generations were molded, by parents, the press, and the
church. If leadership in thinking about social problems is not
to come from the educational institutions, where will it be
found? With the demagogues? Or must the students be left
to run in circles, in a blind effort to find the answers through
their own experience? The only sane answer is that the
experience of the student should receive the guidance of
persons who can bring to bear on the discussion the best
reasoning available in both past and present cultures.

This raises the issue, in educational method, of whether
students should be sheltered from exposure to controversial
questions and from the "isms" proposed as solutions. For
instance, should they be protected from the doctrines of
communism, fascism, anarchism, socialism, or other schemes
for a social reorganization which may be different from our
own system? Should agitators for these various isms be
excluded from the campus? Or should every proposal be
heard and examined irrespective of the emotional heat with
which it may be surrounded?

It is important here to keep sight of the objective of education—development of the power of thinking so that we may use our intelligence to secure the values inherent in democracy. Thinking, as previously indicated, implies developing qualities of discriminating judgment, of respect for facts, of toleration for the opinions of others, and of discipline in the process of analysis and synthesis. Tempering of judgment does not come through ignoring or evading issues or unpleasant facts. It comes rather with facing them, and hauling them into the laboratory for dissection and critical analysis. The student who has not heard a radical agitator until after graduating from college will not be a discriminating leader in scrutinizing the agitator's claims and verifying his facts.

Another aspect of the same question is that we can't be too sure that we have always found the perfect answer to every problem. In fact, we know we haven't. And in the more controversial of the present fields, just as in the days of Galileo in science, we must be sure that we do not stifle freedom of inquiry. To quote Charles Sanders Peirce, "Do not block the way of inquiry."[1] By whom should that inquiry be made if not by those of the best intelligence in society?

A related advantage of free discussion is that it encourages the development of straightforwardness in thought and action, as distinguished from evasiveness. It is the method of relying upon intelligence and intellectual integrity. "Hush-hush" or suppression does not solve the problem; it merely drives discussion underground. Like disease germs, unsound ideas can often best be dealt with by exposing them to the open air of free inquiry and to the sunlight of man's intelligence.

---

[1] Charles Sanders Peirce, *Collected Papers*—Vol. I, *Principles of Philosophy*, p. 56. Cambridge, Mass.: Harvard University Press, 1931.

Furthermore, the examination of controversial issues is a first step toward their solution. The mere fact of controversy shows that there are opposing groups, who have cherished beliefs, privileges, and rights. Progress toward a solution means injury to the rights of certain individuals or groups. And this knowledge must temper the whole process of examination and action. But the criterion cannot be the welfare of particular groups; it must be some higher objective for the society as a whole, such as tends to produce the greatest amount of total human happiness or advancement.

Without some such policy as this toward critical inquiry, the institution will be reduced to voicing slogans and perpetuating dogmas; its intellectual integrity will be debauched with compromise and surrender.

A more specific question for the college to determine is what kind and how much research it proposes to foster. No one would question that the university has a dual function—education and research; but what about the college? What place does research have in a college program, and what should be its function? Some educators argue that a college of liberal arts should not attempt to undertake research, that its particular contribution to education lies in teaching. Others contend that no individual should try to teach on the college level unless he is himself actively at work on the frontier of knowledge.

It may be said that there are two types of research. One is general research—a continuously active inquiry into all aspects of life, an attempt to define and refine one's own philosophical concept of life or of particular phases of life. The second is the special or technical type of research, and refers to specific studies where original inquiry attempts to extend the scope of human knowledge. This second, narrower definition is what the academically trained man ordinarily means by the term "research." In addition to types of research, there is a further point to be considered—the method of research, as distinguished from that of relying on absolutes.

Some individuals have greater aptitude for systematic inquiry than others, although ability in research is in part a matter of disciplined habit. Other individuals have greater aptitude for teaching or counseling, although competence in making critical inquiry and in the use of the scientific method are essential to an adequate analysis of problems and materials and to the training of students in these methods. Presumably, individuals should be used to do what they can do best. Some capable research workers make exceedingly bad teachers, and some stimulating counselors can make no headway in research. But as far as the individuals are concerned, it is not a question of all one or all the other. Rather it is a question of blending both functions into one, in so far as that is feasible. The man of outstanding value to the institution is the rare person who is excellent in both roles. His creative work is a constant challenge to the students, and his presentations to the students help him in clarifying his own ideas. In addition, there is the social gain from both phases of his work.

From the standpoint of the institution, the question can be decided on a practical basis. To argue that the college of liberal arts has no business engaging in research is to limit the college program to the dogmatisms and discoveries of the past. It seems more logical to say that wherever there is intelligence competent to make critical inquiry there should be creative activity of the research type. The question is more one of resources and energy than of the relative desirability of research versus no research. There seems little doubt that, if the activity does not too much encroach on the time that should be devoted to the students, creative work on the part of the faculty adds enormously to the atmosphere of productive and serious effort, and the vitality of the teaching. Group research projects for which time in the faculty schedule is allotted are especially valuable here— and more so if they provide opportunity for active student participation.

Concerning the more general research, if it may be called that—the search for a better way of life—this would seem a natural corollary of the whole college endeavor. It is, in fact, what college is about. Specific methods for this search have already been suggested; it should also be noted that the contributions from the technical research can often play a valuable part in the general program, and that the general program can be a stimulation toward research in specialized problems.

Finally, the method of research—the experimental approach to the study of problems, the attitude of critical inquiry—should be utilized throughout the institution. It is the only way that the student can make knowledge his own: by discovering it—even with guidance—for himself. College for him should be an adventure, a search for a better way of life.

CHAPTER IX

MAKING EDUCATION DYNAMIC

HUMAN society is dynamic. It constantly changes—progresses toward a better group life or retrogresses. Democracy assumes that man, by the use of his intelligence, can help direct and determine the changes which take place. Two factors are involved: thinking and acting. Social progress, therefore, must come through thought in action—i.e., be dynamic. Since it is the concern of education to aid people in developing the qualities which will secure social progress, education itself must be dynamic in its methods.

The older educational goal of producing a cultured man was inherently static; it was an outgrowth of one basic objective of the college, that of passing on the cultural heritage. When in time the possession of this "culture" became a badge of social privilege, this approach to education largely lost its social usefulness.

A more recently developed concept was that of the "rounded man," a broader idea which fixed attention on personal development beyond the mere accumulation of cultural knowledge. But this idea, too, was essentially static in relation to social needs, although, admittedly, attention to health, personality adjustment, and so forth helps pave the way for future action.

Nor does merely adding the study of contemporary social problems to a curriculum endeavoring to produce well-rounded men and women solve the problem. For refined individuals having knowledge of society's greatest needs are not alone the stuff of which democracy is made. There is one further step in the process of educating—inducing action toward human progress, of turning thought into action.

Thinking is an indivisible process, but it can be analyzed in terms of certain stages or phases. There is, for instance, the arousing of an interest and the more specific definition of the interest. There is the observation and collection of data, or the organization of data already in hand. Then follows analysis, the breaking down of the data and ideas, and synthesis, the rebuilding of the material in line with the most promising hypothesis. Finally, conclusions reached or results obtained are communicated in the form of ideas or of action.

Obviously, thinking does not become of social significance until it has been communicated to others or acted upon in some form. Otherwise what is called "thinking" falls into the category of daydreaming. And it is unnecessary to provide educational institutions to induce daydreaming in youth!

Action therefore is an essential. But how to educate for action, when individuals vary greatly not only in intelligence, but in physical make-up, and in aptitudes and talents? Even so, certain preparations for action are common needs of everyone. If ideas are to be communicated, for instance, a vocabulary must be built and added to, and expression in speech or in writing perfected. It follows that attention to the skills of speaking and writing is a requisite for all persons.

When we come to the special talents possessed by individuals, other educational provisions are necessary. The more definitely these talents can be discovered and then utilized as media of action, the more constructive will be the results, individually and socially. The special talents may, of course, be distinctive to the particular individual. They may be physical—size, vigor, stamina, or muscular co-ordination; sensitivity to colors, proportions, arrangements, or harmonies of various kinds; retentive memory, quickness of perception, ability to use symbols; special abilities in dealing with other people. They may involve any of the whole range of intellectual and physical activities. No two people have exactly the same combination of talents and abilities. The educational program should be sufficiently varied and individualized to permit these special qualities to be developed.

Nearly every action we take, however, has some social significance. In nearly all actions, but especially in the achievement of group objectives—that is, in getting the maximum values from group strength—a further development of skills, common to all, is needed. These are the abilities of leadership and "followership." To meet fully the assumed criterion of the good society, people must be willing and prepared to meet the responsibilities of leadership consistent with the talents they possess, and be equally ready and willing to follow and to co-operate when social values supersede individual desires.

These considerations have additional educational implications. One implication is that, for the sake of the individual, the educational process should not be merely the inculcation of the knowledge of the past. The error lies not with the value of this knowledge, but with the method, which is passive. All the student has to do, so to speak, is to open his mouth. If we are trying instead to produce a thinking and acting person, he has to be taught how to search for knowledge on his own, how to utilize this knowledge in the thinking process, and *then how to apply the results of this thinking in life's activities for some individual or social purpose.*

The research method, then—the method of experimentation, which is becoming the chief instrument of human progress—is also the most valuable method in education. Not only does it increase our fund of knowledge—and an institution of higher learning has this as one of its functions; equally important, the research experience is the experience of learning how to think. The method, therefore, as far as the student is concerned, helps teach him not only how to acquire knowledge, but—since one successful hypothesis immediately leads to another—the habit of coupling his thinking with action.

This method is a method of personal experience. Education may be said to be trying to secure change in individuals. Experience is the great factor in producing change. Every experience brings change. Experience is the process of change —of advancement or of retrogression. As William James said, "Experience is a process that continually gives us new material to digest."[1]

Since some experiences are more educative than others, and since change can operate either forward or backward from the standpoint of individual and social values, it is important that the educational institution take stock of the experiences the student is having. This means something more than merely observing, or even supervising, the immediate experiences. It implies thoughtful determination of the

[1] William James, *The Meaning of Truth*, p. 61. New York: Longmans, Green and Company, 1909.

kinds of experiences best suited to the educational ends in view, and the guidance of the student into those avenues of experience.

Educational experience, as John Dewey points out, must be directed. There must be a framework, an educational set-up, in which the experience may be secured. The proposed experiences must be likely to meet the individual and social needs already discussed—that is, to pave the way for the good society. More specifically, they must provide opportunities for the observing, collecting, analyzing, and classifying of facts and ideas, for the testing of ideas and the verification of theories in practice, for the determination of interests, and the definition of these interests in terms of their value individually and socially, and for the acquisition of methods and habits of overcoming inertia and arriving at action.

Educational experience should aim at producing discriminating judgment, which is one of the cornerstones of democracy. And of first importance is the discrimination between social and antisocial values. If we are to achieve progress toward the society which permits the individual to express his personality fully and at the same time secures for the social group the largest advantages of group endeavor, a determination of what helps and what hinders this end must go on continuously. Discrimination of judgment is part and parcel of freed intelligence.

Another significant value is respect for facts. Thinking and acting can hardly achieve the best results unless they are based upon accurate and adequate knowledge. The individual must learn not only how to collect and analyze information; he must acquire the habit of approaching all facts in an attitude of critical inquiry, and of using them experimentally to find out whether they work. This is both the antidote for propaganda and the means of achieving genuine progress.

Finally, thought in action springs most readily from interest and motivation. These qualities may be derived from many sources, but broad and effective interest probably most often arises out of experience, and motivation out of successful experience. In any event, one of the best means of securing interest is through experience. If we consider that little change of educational value takes place unless the individual is interested, we see how interest becomes the starting point for educational effort. Not only is it the starting point; it acts continually as a catalyst. Or, to change the metaphor, interest is the spark plug that touches off thought into action.

Education, therefore, needs to aim at a broader target. Instead of doing something for individuals, or giving them something, education should explore for the innate possibilities in young people, and then so direct their efforts that they become searchers after knowledge and self-motivated to grow. And here, as the old saw has it, experience may be one of the most effective teachers.

CHAPTER X

EXPERIENCE AS A FACTOR IN EDUCATION

A DISTINGUISHING characteristic of the educational program proposed in this book is its use of experience in all phases of college life. The theoretical bases for the use of experience have already been indicated, and have, of course, been fully developed by Froebel, Dewey, and other writers on educational philosophy. It may be helpful here to outline the ways that experience may be practically utilized.

First of all let us consider what experience does *not* mean in this connection. It does *not* refer to a program of activities in the usual popular sense, or as interpreted by some of the more extreme of the progressive schools. It does *not* imply incessant social activities, parties, bull sessions, and entertainments. It is *not* learning to work with the hands, although working with the hands may be of considerable importance. Vocational adjustment on the college level does *not* refer to the learning of trades or manual skills—although these may be assets, vocational or avocational, or "ladder rungs" in the ascent toward positions of leadership. Far from encouraging the extroverts through activities to become more extroverted, the college, through knowing them well, should attempt to harness their drives and turn them in more balanced and productive directions.

The idea advocated here is to use experience as one of the primary methods in developing the whole personality, which includes increasing the ability to think effectively and to couple the thinking of the individual with his acting and living. The aim is to make the learning process more genuine, more meaningful to the student, and to teach him how to make his thinking on social problems applicable to the culture in which he lives.

In realizing these ends, experience should not be something tacked onto the academic program, for use in leisure time; it should be, instead, one of the threads which draw the whole program together into unity, operating in all phases of the curriculum as well as in extraclass activities.

In the academic program itself, the student gains one type of experience through working out his own ideas by way of experimentation and research. Lectures are useful for orientation, interpretation, or the addition of otherwise unavailable information. But the old-time methods of lecture and recitation, already emphasized less than formerly by the colleges, and the rigid system of three to five meetings a week for parroting the textbook, should be largely discontinued. For they are too much the mere practice of a skill—memorizing—and the practice of it in a detrimental way—the retention of information only until the examination has been passed.

Instead, the curriculum should be sufficiently flexible to permit the use of any one of the numerous methods available, or combinations of them. But the college should always keep in mind that it is the student who is there to learn, and that the education offered him ought to become an integral part of his life. This means more use of the methods of the laboratory, more discussions on significant problems, greater emphasis on independent theses, on reading, and on the questioning and discussion possible in the personal or small-group conferences. It implies the use of such aids as the course syllabus, which will cut the apron string of daily assignments and encourage the student to pursue his studies independently. It suggests achievement examinations for large areas of knowledge, increasingly complex as the student progresses in college, to determine his genuine and lasting accomplishments and his ability to draw upon the knowledge of numerous fields in solving a particular problem.

In other words, as a part of the academic procedure, the desire is to teach the student the research method: to tackle a problem with self-confidence and to search out the vital information, analyze it, and determine upon conclusions which seem valid to him. College should teach the student methods he can continue to use when he no longer has instructors at hand to guide him.

Along with the academic work, two other areas of experience have more potential educational value for the student than is commonly realized. One of them is the area of extraclass activities. Ordinarily these activities are permitted to thrive, subject to the pruning shears of regulation. Instead of being merely tolerated, they should be grasped as a positive instrument of education and planned as a way to make the campus a laboratory in living. This distinction may be subtle, but it is vital; it means replacing the negative by the positive approach in this area of the educational experience. For it cannot be denied that through these campus activities many students learn more things which receive active expression in their lives than they learn in the classroom—witness the college-trained political manipulator or the college-bred social butterfly; or, on the positive side, the student government leader become community and national leader. The educational objective, then, is to give these activities the guidance and direction of the faculty; more than that, to encourage the students themselves to use this time, not alone for fun, but to gain both individual and group values otherwise unattainable. A basic factor here is giving students responsibility as a means of securing personal growth in character and capacity for leadership. An important feature is the planning of activities so that every student can be induced to participate; for it is often the student who most needs the benefits of these activities who neglects them most (or is most neglected by them) under the unplanned system.

The second additional area of experience referred to is off-campus activities. The off-campus program should give the stimulation of a wider, richer, and more realistic environment than that possible for the campus. Both the scope and the intensity of observations, and the accuracy with which they must be made when one applies theory to practice, have a direct relationship to the quality of the thinking of the individual. It is the writer's observation, for example, that in examinations the students who have had these off-campus experiences approach the questions with a spirit of critical analysis not commonly shown by those lacking the experience. Another habit gained is that of coming to conclusions or of making decisions. Job experience necessitates testing conclusions in practice, and thus a greater discrimination in judgment is secured.

A good example of the use of experience or personal

activity comes from the athletic program. There seems little of genuine educational advantage in a program of professionalized athletics. In so far as they absorb an unduly large proportion of the energies available for athletics, their effect is to put 99 per cent of the students among the spectators. The cheering may be activity and good recreation, but hardly designed for intellectual enlightenment. But this topic has been adequately treated by others; also it seems one of the phases of the college program least susceptible to reform. What is important is that all students, the least athletically inclined even more than the all-American football player, should get some of the values that athletics has to offer. This can, of course, be accomplished through a well-planned intramural program of sports and games. Additional values will be gained if health and recreation is integrated with the rest of the college program as one of the many means toward the development of the whole personality.

Still another example comes from the active arts program. Although the colleges are called "liberal arts" colleges, art both as courses in the field and especially as creative activity has tended to disappear from the liberal program and become instead a hothouse plant in the conservatory. The financial reason may weigh heavily here, since frequently this phase of the college program is supported in whole or in large part by additional fees charged the students. Probably it is also a part of the trend to develop highly specialized schools—and for some reason, the specialized training of artists and musicians has not received as much criticism from college faculties as has specialized training in other fields. But the fact remains that the average student of the liberal college has little contact with the active arts. True, a small clique of students may participate intensively in dramatics, or those on the debating team may spend most of their time in this activity, or those who can play instruments may join, or be dragged into, the orchestra. Consequently, the college has these activities on the campus—but for the specialized benefit of relatively small groups of individuals, and largely for the entertainment, as spectators, of the remainder of the students and faculty.

The arts in some form should be a natural part of the activities of all students. The individual who has had the least contact with them in his previous environment may be the one most needing this experience in his college period. Art is a phase of self-expression; everyone needs to acquire the skills and qualities inherent in the creative activities. And rightly organized, these activities can offer opportunity for nearly every kind of creative talent. For example, the writing, staging, and producing of plays is as important an activity as the acting in them. All levels of education have something to learn from the nursery and progressive elementary schools when it comes to the methods of teaching art, and the use of art education for bringing out the creative talents in students.

What, then, is the objective of using experience in education? It is to arouse greater interest, to secure greater emotional drive, to get the habit and skill of critical inquiry, to improve the quality and power of thinking and acting or living. These claims are too broad to make for experience alone. The claim is, rather, that directed experience can be used to help secure for the student some of the driving power and the intellectual and emotional "edge" which are distinguishing characteristics of the creative or productive individual. Experience as an implement of education teaches the student how to get the full meaning out of experience—as the preparation for his doing the same thing throughout the remainder of his life.

CHAPTER XI

THE CAMPUS, A LABORATORY IN LIVING

THE principle that preparing for the future can best be done by learning how to live fully and successfully in the ever-continuing present has been fully enunciated by leading educators and already discussed here. What is here emphasized is the dynamic rather than the static—the thinking rather than the daydreaming—the active, productive, or creative, rather than the passive or parasitical—individual.

One of the values sought in this proposed educational program is deriving from and for society the advantages and values inherent in group association and endeavor. The desire to do this, comprehension of the possibilities, and skill in achieving this objective should be among the marks of the educated man. Directed experience is the best way of acquiring the necessary abilities and habits. Presumably these habits and abilities can best be acquired during the formative years, as of the college period. For these reasons, in planning the college program, we should consider ways and means of providing experiences which serve these ends.

Fortunately, there is no inherent reason why the college must maintain an artificial environment secluded from the main currents of life. Indeed, the less isolation the better. Normal life experiences constitute the natural foundation for the educational program; the world in which the student lives, and will continue to live, is his best laboratory.

The college, then, can be defined as a laboratory for learning how to live more fully. It is something more than an educational plant in which absent-minded professors lecture three times a week about the cultural heritage of the past. The college period should be a live, vital, dynamic experience—a necessary period of development in the life of the individual of intellectual caliber. Only in that it is planned especially to offer educational advantages is it artificial; most of its activity is a normal part of living, and the remainder should be composed of normal experiences carried into the laboratory to be dissected, examined, and evaluated in terms of the more perfect life.

If the best society is that society which permits to the individual the opportunity to develop most fully the potentialities of his personality and which at the same time gains for all individuals the greatest possible advantages from group strength, it is a function of education to help find the essential elements in this equation, and to aid individuals in getting the outlook, motivation, discrimination in judgment, and skill in creative action necessary to solving the equation. Planning the program is, then, in part, discovering methods of fulfilling this function. There may be many ways to accomplish the purpose; but the essential is to see the significance of the objective and to participate actively in the search. Presumably the search should be something more than speculative effort; it should be in part the process of experimentation, of trial and error, in the community laboratory.

In general, there have been two concepts of the best

college community for educational purposes. One is that the environment should be secluded from distractions, and purified of annoying or contaminating influences. The extreme example is the monastery where the student of life speculates upon life from a distance. An attitude formerly widespread among colleges is well-expressed in the following quotation from the regulations of a Methodist college (Cokesbury) of 1792: ". . . All in our College . . . [shall] be kept at the utmost distance as from vice in general, so in particular from softness and effeminacy of manners. We shall therefore inflexibly insist on their rising early in the morning—Only one shall bathe at a time; and no one shall remain in the water above a minute . . . The students shall be indulged with nothing which the world calls *play*. Let this rule be observed with the strictest nicety; for those who play when they are young, will play when they are old."[1] Although colleges no longer go to this extreme, many still use a paternalistic system, regulating the students' lives for them and busily shooing away "evil" influences.

In this method are at least two fundamental detriments to the educational objective. In the first place, the system needed to carry out this concept is the old familiar one of inculcation and administrative discipline. The self-defeating effect of absolute standards, authoritarian doctrines, and imposed disciplinary methods in education has already been noted. It means that the student needs only to memorize the rules, be a good boy, and follow the example of his elders.

[1] W. H. Kilpatrick, *Source Book in the Philosophy of Education*, pp. 4, 5. New York: The Macmillan Company, 1924.

The paternalistic approach tends to close the door to thought and action in a vital sphere of life. Furthermore, it is frequently negative in its influence, as witness the resulting hypocrisy when a church school has strong rules against dancing and the faculty knowingly winks at flagrant violations. The unfortunate effect of the system on the faculty is to push them into the role of preachers, detectives, and often hypocrites.

In the second place, the method rules out the very materials which would be the most useful in promoting discriminating thinking and socially productive action. For out of the wealth of problems that flow across the college campus arises an excellent opportunity to define social and antisocial values. Here again are natural educational situations, with sufficiently concrete application to the individual's own life to assure his interest and careful thought. They give him, literally, something to think about.

These remarks suggest the next point. The second, what may be called the emerging, concept of the best kind of college community is that it is a laboratory in living. Students and faculty together search for the best way of life. Instead of being presented with predigested ideas, each new generation of students helps formulate the concepts of the good life. There is nothing in this method that prevents the individual, faculty or student, from having definite views about morals, ethics, purposes, and perfections; indeed, such views are essential. But it does assume that these ideas are not absolutes to be imposed upon all who may happen to be subordinate to one in position. It assumes, further, that the faculty, too, have not yet found the last word; they are themselves still growing intellectually and are pursuing their own researches and further education. Finally, it assumes the experimental, reasoning approach to truth.

Here, again, the important result is not the amount of knowledge learned or quantity of ideas inculcated, but the rate and direction of growth of the individual. For the community, too, the valuable thing is not one particular form of environment, but the progress being made in working toward the ideal. Too often, inculcation and indoctrination result in compromised mediocrity. A shared quest for the good life will at least arouse interest, discussion, and activity, and may bring about a genuinely superior mode of community living.

Again, this is not to advocate the abandonment of all codes and all ideals. The reverse is really true. It is merely that the search of the students and faculty for the highest ideals should not be too much inhibited or restricted by imposed regulations. Regulations limit the educational influence. A richer educational experience in defining ideals would seem to lie in examining contemporary codes in the light of all available human experience and thinking, past and present.

The use of the campus as a laboratory brings specific values which tie in with the educational results desired from the college program as a whole. When problems are discussed openly and an attempt is made to solve them on the basis of sound reasoning, the individual participates in the thinking process. The answer is not handed to him; he must help find it. And since there are no predetermined answers, he must help verify the solution by further trial and error. The procedure, then, is typical of the experimental method. The interest that can be created has already been remarked; with interest comes also motivation, and a feeling of responsibility for action.

Moreover, the absence of detailed regulations of action forces the student to make choices of his own. Will his individual action be social or antisocial? What *is* social and antisocial? What is the best course of action for him to pursue, and why? The answer is that the individual must use his own intelligence, not someone else's, in determining what to do. The thinking, however, need not be a purely individual activity since the whole of the campus is thinking about the same situations and is making choices and judgments. In particular, the faculty counselors, if they have an adequate understanding of the students, can play an active part in stimulating and directing this thinking.

Social pressures are a natural part of life; obviously, they are still present under this system. But the pressure is not that of authority. Neither is it the undermining and evasion of college rules and regulations. The social pressure comes in part from the spirit and tone of the campus. It is the spirit of adventure, of inquiry, of co-operation, of confidence —of striving to attain the greatest individual freedom consistent with the best social values. The pressure comes also in part from the surrounding community, which thus helps maintain an orientation of the *ideal* toward the *actual* state of society. For if young people are to become leaders in their communities, they must have a realistic knowledge and sympathetic understanding of how these communities feel.

Far from being anarchy, the method involves carefully organized planning. The goal of the more perfect society indicates direction; but the process of getting there takes continuous planning by individuals and by the group as a whole. The program demands active leadership by the faculty. It also requires group organization designed to secure student participation and responsibility.

An individual advantage is that the students tend to become self-starting, self-disciplining, maturing persons. Is this not the obvious goal for the man of intelligence? And the group, too, will learn how to move toward solving its common problems and toward seeking better ways to solve them. Students thus learn how the method of thought in action may be used to arrive at higher social values from group endeavor. The individual learns that the group is more than the sum of its parts, that something larger and finer results when there is co-operative pooling of finances, efforts, and ideas.

In devising a campus laboratory of this kind, one must of course define the principles upon which it is based. These have been implicit in the discussion already given, but will again be briefly analyzed.

First of all, the individual and social goals inherent in this thesis include the development of the whole personality of the individual, and the search for higher social values. Basic to both is the utilization of incidents and problems, individual and social, arising naturally in life, as educational situations. It is implied that all problems and all aspects of life will come under consideration, whether controversial or not, and that the solutions sought will be based upon intelligence and reason and will be accepted as bases for life actions.

Secondly, there is the principle that the program shall be both individualized and socialized. This is apparent when we consider what we want to reach as the more perfect society. It is also essential as educational technique. For it is the individual who is becoming educated, and his growth has to start from where he is and proceed as far as his needs, interests, and capacities will take him. This cannot well happen when students are viewed and dealt with in the mass. The socialization of the program lies in its endeavor to search for and secure the best advantages possible in group living.

In the third place, there is the idea of planned versus unplanned program. Since a program is a plan, this thought may seem redundant. But the idea emphasizes the specific individual, either faculty or student, who needs the opportunity to participate in the planning; and the expansion of that planning beyond the academic curriculum to all aspects of the campus environment and life. Individual participation means that the planning is a continuous process—the moment a "set" of any kind occurs, to that extent education stops. This flexibility and fluidity should be a characteristic of the educational institution, although to some extent it is a prerequisite in any society that wants to be free. Expansion of planning refers to the educational advantages of having student life and campus activities become an integral part of the college program, rather than of regarding them as poor relations, tolerated but hardly welcomed.

Finally, there is the principle of the faculty-student shared quest for a better way of life. This has two aspects: The first is the common participation by both students and faculty. Here the faculty must recognize both their responsibility and their opportunity. The excuse will be advanced that valuable time will thus be taken from the academic work; but this fails to recognize that campus living can be as much a part of giving the student a liberal education as the classroom is. The excuse reflects also the rationalization whereby people of high intelligence, who should be most productive in action, so frequently avoid community responsibilities and fail to grasp the opportunity of working toward the larger group values possible in society. The second aspect of the "shared quest" idea is that, through it, authoritarian dictates are superseded by a search for a better way of life on the individual's own initiative and by his own desire.

These principles need some further elaboration to indicate the way this community laboratory can be made to operate effectively. It is, of course, necessary as a first step to scrap the negative features of the old system—the system of rules, penalties, and so forth. The approach to the new plan is always the positive approach of reasoned consideration of objectives, principles, and possible methods. And the assumption should be that the plan is based upon intelligence and reasoning in action. Narrow social pressures are examined by a reasoning process, and a continuous effort is made to define and refine standards and to secure changed action consistent with the results of this thinking. The mechanism of the plan is different from the old in that, instead of the individual's being condemned or penalized by the institution for the violation of rules, the new method permits incidents which counselors, more mature students, or the group as a whole consider antisocial to be seized upon as opportunities to make the individual realize the possibilities in higher standards of action. The reasoning of the counselor is thus pitted against the reasoning of the individual in question, presumably with some educational results.

It is not implied here that there shall be no rules. In a college there are some matters concerning which it is useful to have regulations, and others where they tend to defeat the educational purpose. The former, like traffic rules, promote the functioning of the group and thus aid in achieving the primary purpose of the institution. These relate for the most part to procedures and scheduling, but may also cover such points of conduct as the uses to which particular rooms or buildings shall be put, conduct during a fire drill, and so forth. Sometimes they are regulations putting into effect minimum standards, the meeting of which is essential for admission to, or continuance with, the faculty-student group —standards in academic performance, in health, in the basic relationships between the sexes, in social living, or in any other areas important to the environment or to achieving the over-all purposes of the institution. Here, however, the objective is not regulating the lives of the students and faculty; instead, it is so planning the program that all individuals are better able to achieve good standards, and the college can better accomplish its purposes. The place where rules tend to defeat the educational purpose is where intellectual discrimination is important, the areas in which personal behavior or group activities should be determined on the basis of intelligence and reason rather than through authoritative regulation. Regulation substitutes the thinking of the administrators or faculty for the thinking of the students; and students, as we have said, cannot become educated unless they are permitted to think, and carry their thinking into action.

To facilitate the task of administration, it may be useful to make a distinction between rules and standards. Rules are formulated by the appropriate governmental unit and applied administratively; they are definite in their requirements, although it is doubtful whether the college should attempt to enforce them by exacting penalties. Even here, an effort should be made to secure adherence to them on the basis of reason—the fact that nonadherence defeats the purposes of the group as a whole; and repeated lack of co-operation is evidence that the individual is not sufficiently interested in those purposes to warrant his remaining with the group. Logically, the one penalty should be a request to withdraw from the college.

Standards are not regulations. They may or may not be formulated, but if formulated they should be stated as purposes, principles, and ideals. When formulated, they should be redefined repeatedly, since the object of defining them is to secure group thinking about what constitutes the most desirable way of life on the campus.

There are two levels of standards: those which exist as the present mode of community actions; and those which represent the formulated goals for the community. Since the formulated standards, if democratically determined, obviously represent the result of group thinking about particular problems, the real test of the educational results—the consistency of thought and action—comes through examining how closely the actual standards check with the formulated ones.

There is also a distinction between community standards and personal standards. The standards of an individual may be below or above those of the community. What should be asked of the individual is that he will live by the standards which accord with his own intellectual integrity. Because the environmental background of the students varies widely, individuals will of necessity be applying widely varying standards in their actions. But the practice of fidelity to their own views provides the very opportunity which the institution is seeking—that of bringing to their attention the incidents and problems, or evidences of achievement, which in the more discriminating judgments of the counselors are either social or antisocial, good or bad, and which provide points of focus for educational effort. If the standards of the individual fall consistently below the regulations (minimum standards) of the college, and reasonable effort with him fails to secure interest and improvement, he should simply be asked to withdraw from the college.

If we dismiss morals momentarily from our minds and draw an illustration from scholarship, we can see these distinctions more objectively. Where "4" represents a perfect cumulative grade average, "2.1" frequently represents the minimum passing average. The grade of "2.1" is therefore a regulation. No student can be graduated who falls below this point. The actual standard or mode of the institution, however, may be "2.5," although there is no formulation of this except as the historical record reveals it. The college may not be content with its standards, and the students and faculty agree to pull together to raise them to some other level, such as "3.0." This figure of "3.0" then becomes a formulated standard toward which the group pressure will be focused. The individual, in turn, has intellectual standards of his own which are the result of his past habits and sensitivities. If his intellectual standards are materially below those desired by the group, his counselors and the appropriate committee, under the standards system, will work with him in the effort to awaken his interest and to reform his study habits accordingly.

In an institution of higher learning which sets out to fulfill the social function of liberal education as we have defined it, the education of students in ethical outlook and social relationships is fundamentally important. Hence, the same reasoning about regulations and standards applies in these areas as applies to scholarship. The object of both is the same—to secure educational growth.

The social actions of students are sometimes annoying and inconvenient. Occasionally they are shocking to the next older generation—and this applied just as much to the "bloomer girls" of grandmother's day as it does to the present generation. But the thing that really matters is the direction in which the student is growing. Environment is such a big factor in determining that direction that the campus needs to work continuously at orienting the environment toward socially enduring values. The educational process then becomes one of continuously securing change in the students toward more social attitudes, beliefs, and actions. This is an essential part of the search for a better way of life.

This method, of course, is not without its limitations in practice, usually because of the presence in the student group of individuals who are not seriously interested in improving their ideas and habits of life. Often, too, the pressure of parents and of the local community will put limitations on the experimentation in human behavior. The answer to the "playboy" student would seem to be that if he doesn't exhibit any sincere desire to become educated, he should, after reasonable effort with him, be asked to leave the institution. The liberal college is not a reform school—the untractable boy belongs in a school geared to meet his needs. But with practically all students, the "campus laboratory" environment produces response rather than rebellion. The answer to the parents or pressure groups in society depends upon the relative importance of the matter under consideration. Good public relations are essential for the continued existence of the educational program; hence reasonable conformance to customs is indicated. But in so far as this conformance tends to regulate individual activities, it should be governed by definite principles. One is that the group, as a whole or through some representative agency, decides after due consideration upon its course of action; and the second is that there should be some principles of such fundamental value to the group—civil liberties, for example—that the members should be willing to go down with colors flying, if need be, rather than to yield to social pressures. How tragic it was that the German universities following 1932 failed to take a firm stand for principles in which they believed!

The usual method of attempting to achieve these objectives is through establishing a student government. The reasoning behind this effort was well-stated by Charles W. Eliot:

Student self-government or student participation in school or college government conforms to three of the most fundamental principles of education—principles too often neglected, even by persons whose lives are devoted to educational service.

The first of these fundamental principles is that the real object in

education so far as the development of character is concerned, is
to cultivate in the child a capacity for self-control or self-government,
not a habit of submission to an overwhelming, arbitrary, external
power, but a habit of obeying the dictates of honor and duty, as
enforced by active will power within the child.

The second fundamental principle, to which properly conducted
self-government seems to me to conform, is that in childhood and
in youth it is of the utmost importance to appeal steadily, and almost
exclusively, to motives which will be operative in after life. In too
much of our systematic education, we appeal to motives which we
are sure cannot last; to motives which may answer for little children
of six, ten or twelve, but which are entirely unapplicable to boys
or girls of fourteen, sixteen or eighteen. Thus, the motive of fear
is one of these transitory motives on which organized education in
the past has almost exclusively relied; yet it is well determined by
the history of the race that the fear of punishment, whether in this
world or the next, is a very ineffective motive with adults.

The third fundamental principle in education is Froebel's doctrine
that children are best developed through productive activities, that
is, through positive, visible achievement in doing, making, or producing something.

Student self-government enforces positive activity; it appeals
steadily to motives in the boys which will serve them when they
become men; and it is constantly trying to develop in the boyish
community the capacity of self-government. Therefore, I say it is
based on sound educational principles.[2]

Student self-government is undoubtedly a step in the right
direction. It is excellent as a method if the government is
given sufficient freedom and responsibility so that it will not
always be dealing with inconsequentials and with matters
on the periphery of what the community is really trying
to achieve. But it is obvious that student government in
practice is not permitted to do the job which Dr. Eliot

[2] This quotation was taken from a leaflet issued by the National Self-
Government Committee, Inc., 80 Broadway, New York.

envisioned; nor can students working alone achieve such an objective.

What is needed is some mechanism to bring faculty and students together. This is important for several reasons: the typical campus problems are of common concern to faculty and students, and need the unified attention of a single group; the segregation of students into a student government is deficient as a method because ordinarily the students are permitted only nominal authority and responsibility; and in the light of the primary educational purpose involved, it is of the essence that the faculty be in some relationships to student problems through which they can stimulate, counsel, and instruct. Student government as it is commonly practiced should therefore be eliminated; and a new form of social organization, including all members of the institution, should be created. This would be a community government. The Antioch College Community Government,[3] for example, is modeled after the commission-manager form of municipal government. But it is not alone a "government" in the narrow sense; it is in reality an extension of the classroom, in part a redefinition of the classroom; it is at the same time part and parcel of the counseling program. It not only ties in these aspects of the college program with its own objectives, but also serves as a particular organization through which to search for the best means of harmonizing individual freedom with group endeavors.

Faculty participation does not need to rob the students of their prerogatives. It should have the opposite effect,

---

[3] See the bulletin, *Of, By, and For—A Study in the Democratic Method*, Antioch College, Yellow Springs, Ohio (1938); also, *Practicing Democracy in the College*, Pamphlet No. 8, Education and National Defense Series, U.S. Office of Education (1942).

bringing active student participation into a much wider area of college responsibilities than the usual peripheral ones handled by student government. And, as I have already suggested, the faculty are placed in a natural teaching situation. One administrative principle involved is to give authority and expect responsibility. Defining that responsibility involves again the process of reasoning. With the assumption of responsibility comes discriminating judgment and the other values which arise through experience.

It is also necessary to decide what the student-faculty organization shall have jurisdiction over. Some of the obvious tasks of a college administration concern the formulation of program, the changes in personnel, and the provision and maintenance of facilities and other factors in environment. Practically speaking, the question arises: Which of these functions have greater and which lesser educational possibilities? The answer cannot be given arbitrarily. For instance, what goes into the curriculum should interest both students and faculty, but the scheduling of procedures would seem of necessity to be delegated to administrative experts. What constitutes successful teaching needs mutual understanding, but the teachers of a subject should have the freedom to define the content of the course and the responsibility of the students in the course. There are phases of community life which obviously are of common interest to both faculty and students: the social life, the sports and recreational program, the active arts—music, dramatics, publications—and the provision of co-operative services such as food, supplies, medical attention, and insurance against fire, accident, and illness.

Participation in some of these activities may have specific

as well as general advantages. In the formulation of educational policy, for example, occasionally the faculty and almost always the students are excluded. Yet even with the students, having to define individual and social needs and to set up general and specific goals aids greatly in clarifying and in broadening the individual's own goals. In addition, since educational policy constitutes one of the broad social problems suggested as the basis for the general curriculum, making the immediate institutional problem a part of the laboratory content serves the purpose of applying thought and action to a concrete situation of more than ordinary interest to the participant.

One of the possibilities in the community laboratory is the use of the necessary community services—such as food, supply, and insurance—to study methods of co-operation and to appraise the relative values in competition and in co-operation as ways of supplying these services. Still another possibility lies in the governmental organization itself. Here is an opportunity to find out what forms of government secure the best possible adjustment in individual and group relationships, in setup and methods of administration, and in using the machinery of government for securing added group advantages. The cry of our times for better methods of training for citizenship in a democracy is usually met by adding courses of study in the theory and practice of government. These are fine as far as they go, but they do not include the necessary educational ingredients of experimentation and experience, which lead to motivation, discrimination in judgment, and skills and habits of action. Students who are being educated for leadership in a democracy should have this directed practice in learning how the democratic method works.

The use of the social life of the campus for laboratory purposes also deserves a word of elaboration. The social life broadly speaking includes three things: recreational activities; avocational interests; and the more individual relationships between—for example—men and women, and the kind of personal conduct which impinges on the rights of others. Here again is needed both the individualization and the socialization of the programs. Individuals need freedom to express their personalities, but this self-expression must not be to the disadvantage of others or undermine the best group objectives. In part, the freedom is absence of unnecessary restriction, but it is in part also the creation of more adequate opportunities for self-expression; and the positive as distinguished from the restricted social program searches out these new opportunities. This, on the one hand, means the enrichment of the community's activities by planned additions and by quality substitutions, and on the other, the devising of methods by which activities are available to every individual either because of his talents or his need in personal advancement. This implies the absence of cliques, arbitrary discriminations, and special privilege based on artificial considerations; and the definite planning of the social program to provide interesting, varied, and educationally sound activities.

It implies also an understanding of the individual and his social relationships on the part of the counselor, an effort to encourage the diffident or nonsocial person, and equal effort to divert the energies and interests of the too-social person into channels more fruitful for his balanced development. Particularly do students need to be stimulated toward new or more rewarding avocational interests.

For several years Antioch College has been experimenting successfully with a plan of community participation. It represents a deliberate effort to improve the quality of the activities on the campus, and to encourage widespread, balanced participation, both in these activities and in the larger community life.

American environment is somewhat lacking in the influences—musical, artistic, recreational, and creative—which enrich society and bring to the individual greater happiness and finer growth in personality. With the coming of more leisure time comes also the need of cultivating leisure-time interests; and in no place is this more pertinent than in the liberal arts college.

A primary use of the social laboratory is in the student's individual relationships and social conduct. Here exist a wealth of situations in which the individual can be reached educationally, and in which he will have to make repeated evaluations of his own interests in relation to those of the group. In addition, the deliberate assignment of responsibilities to the individual in line with his maturity and capacities will develop in him the tempering and molding of attitudes, judgment, and action which ordinarily come only with experience. Directed experiences of this type would seem a much surer way of developing fine character than the method of indoctrination and restricted freedom. The community, also, has a much healthier basis in individual responsibility than it has when the college administration shoulders the whole of the responsibility for ensuring moral and ethical action. Another campus objective is to avoid

the minus values of undirected social activities—the growth
of undemocratic influences, the invention of corrupting
political machines, the development of habits of suspicion
and distrust and of cleavages between faculty and students,
and all of the other community weeds which get rooted and
thrive when there is no conscious community attempt to
discriminate between good and bad.

An important part of the mechanism is the use of committees. Committees not only promote democratic discussion
and planning, but constitute focal centers for educative
experience. The traditionally-minded member of the faculty
may frown at the presence of numerous committees on the
campus. He would have good reason to frown if a particular student served on so many committees that he had
no time for other study or experience. But an advantage of
a planned program is that these responsibilities can be
decentralized. A committee then becomes a point of action
for the student—a point at which his thinking materializes
into action which affects the social group. It is an educative
situation in which faculty and students think and act together on some common problem. It is a device for the discovery of potential leadership material, for through the
committee system individuals emerge to assume responsibility. The discovery and training of these leaders—large
numbers of them—is a fundamental objective of the college.
The decentralized committee is a device through which
leadership training can be given to large numbers of the
students.

Supplementing and implementing the formal governmental
setup, there need to be established various educational
methods, such as organized discussion meetings and com-

munity forums. These can be concerned both with major questions and proposals growing out of the activities of the community government, and with the issues confronting the larger community, nation, or society in which the college has its setting. Here again is a tie-in between the work in the community laboratory and the academic program.

These devices—committees, meetings, and forums—are machinery of great importance in a democratic society. Misunderstanding and frictions are the breeding grounds for fascism, the basis for rationalizing the use of the "strong arm" in government. The alternative to dictation is consensus. And consensus *necessitates* techniques for group thinking which produce action that can gain general support. Instruction in these techniques is important for all citizens in a democracy, but especially so for those who may have the capacity to lead.

A final consideration in planning a community laboratory of the type suggested here is that it must have an unusually close understanding between faculty and students. The group, considering its changing composition, needs to keep its objectives clearly defined. In addition to a plan or system, it needs also to foster the kind of spirit that is generated naturally from the attempt to define and realize ideals. The attitude of the faculty is important because it must get and keep the confidence of the students and of fellow faculty. The faculty cannot be moralistic, but must base their proposals upon reasons which they are willing and able to advance. Of greatest importance is their attitude of expecting high performance and attitudes from the students. Young people normally are idealists. Having faced little disillusionment in life, they readily accept trust and respond to expectation. In fact, they arrive at college themselves eager and expectant in their relationships with the faculty.

The basic principle is one of honor in relationships. But something more than the usual "honor system" is required. The honor system as meaning no proctors in the examination room, worthy as it is in theory, has normally small chance of success. For it is tacked onto a system of cleavage between faculty and students, or rules to which intellectual adherence is not given, and of the threat of discipline. It questions per se the presence of honor by requiring the individual to sign a confession that he has been strictly honorable. Now the essence of honor is social responsibility. The important thing involved is not the harm to the particular individual who cheats himself out of an education—he suffers his self-inflicted penalty. The value at stake is the preservation of integrity and of straightforward, dependable action in faculty-student and student-student relationships. If the purposes of the institution are to be achieved, it must preserve an atmosphere in which co-operation is possible. This reasoning makes it apparent that the idea of honor must permeate the whole of the community in all relationships, inside the classroom and out. The achievement of this goal, considering the tremendous differences in environmental backgrounds of the individuals, is itself a matter of education. In practice, it means that the faculty must strongly desire to achieve and maintain this type of campus environment, and exert their influence accordingly.

There are two possible ways of handling campus life and activities. One is the familiar system of arbitrary rules with accompanying penalties for infractions. A variation of this is to let activities grow up and run on a laissez-faire basis, subject only to an occasional crackdown on the part of a major official. Frequently this is the actual state of affairs existing behind a screen of rules. The educational influence is accidental, and may be either good or bad. The second alternative is the one described herein, aimed at definite educational objectives. But it should be borne in mind that the honor system is a "system" and involves continuous and active planning if it too is not to degenerate into laissez faire.

The college community, then, offers great possibilities as an educational laboratory. Some of the supposed disadvantages are apparent rather than genuine. The choice is not between a carefully regulated environment and anarchy. It is rather between two plans for the community, one predetermining the mold into which the students shall fit, and the other utilizing the community for educational purposes to the maximum possible extent. It may be objected that for making the second plan a success there is neither time nor energy available. This argument, in addition to passing over the real objective of the institution, fails to consider the efficiency of a plan based upon honor, which utilizes education to plug some of the holes and root out some of the inefficiencies. Consider, as one small example, the time saved in being able to leave doors unlocked. Finally, the larger objectives of freeing the individual and freeing society apply in college as well as elsewhere. And these purposes may best be achieved for students by teaching them to substitute reason for unguided emotion or hearsay.

CHAPTER XII

IN THE WORLD AND ABOVE IT

A MAN is likely to speak Chinese if he is born in China, believe in Buddha if he is reared in India, and join the Democratic party if he lives in the deep South. The world he comprehends is made up of fishing and hunting, if he is born in a northern igloo; and of factory-made bread, traffic jams, symphony concerts, and round-the-world luxury liners, if he is born in New York. Such is the influence of environment. A horse is pretty much a horse the world over, but a man may vary from the ignorant, superstitious, pack-carrying peon to the harnesser of lightning and the shaper of human destinies. Particular boys may have equal intellectual capacity; but the uses to which they put their intelligence will be determined by the quality and amount of stimulation they receive from their environment. Thus does personal experience shape men's lives.

The college is a particular type of environment, planned to educate. Its objective is twofold: to stimulate the individual to an awareness and development of his own personal potentialities and to educate him concerning the world in which he lives and in thinking clearly and constructively about its problems. In planning the college program one immediately encounters the question: Can these objectives best be sought in a secluded, restricted environment or in one set down at the busy crossroads? Although there have been brilliant exceptions, it can be asserted that neither the monastic life nor the life of random experiences has been conspicuously successful in producing outstanding personalities or creative leaders. Even the Abe Lincoln is usually found to have combined study and reflection with active effort toward creating a better world.

It is obvious that if the college relies too heavily upon experiences in the workaday world as the major element in its program, there will be little to distinguish it from the noncollege environment. On the other hand, if the students are secluded too severely, their studies will lack significance and their thinking will be short of the tempering and disciplining to which it would otherwise be subjected. The educational environment, then, needs to be both above and beyond the practical affairs of life, and yet a part of the world of reality. Participation in the work of the world helps provide an understanding of contemporary culture and of its problems; periods of study and reflection permit the student to examine and apply the wisdom of past cultures, and to gain competence in study and research; further participation serves to test facts and judgments and to redefine principles in the light of experience.

This program therefore favors extending the educational environment of the student to include off-campus experiences under the direction of competent counselors. By off-campus experiences is meant anything that carries the student into active personal observation of, or participation in, community life, current affairs, and practical work. These experiences may come through numerous channels: travel, survey trips and projects, participating in political, civic, and religious activities, and holding actual jobs in industrial, professional, or governmental service. More specific illustrations might include making a survey of community housing, carrying a petition to Washington, or earning a weekly wage in a factory. There is, of course, no absolute dividing line between these experiences and the community-laboratory ones. In a way, both have the same objectives, and may sometimes be identical.

The first value of this kind of experience is that it improves the student's capacity for thinking. Experiences make the classroom theories more concrete and possessed of genuine meaning to the student. The experience enables the student to get fuller value from the ideas discussed; and it is right here—where he begins to comprehend the relation of theory to life as we live it—that the most significant value from education is derived. An essential part of the college environment is the ideas of great thinkers as revealed by books, and the secrets of nature as exposed in the laboratory. These are stimulating to the imagination, and are essential guides and controls for thought; nothing is educationally more valuable. But for the best intellectual understanding of such ideas and facts, they must become tangible in the experience of the individual. Furthermore, assuming that an important goal of education is learning how to transform thought into action, the individual must make his understanding genuine in the sense of expressing it in his own life activities.

There will be no difference of opinion, for instance, over the proposal that in the classroom the abstract idea of justice should receive speculative consideration. And it will be agreed that a student will emerge from the classroom with some new and stimulating ideas. But it should be recognized that for him the idea will remain abstract and nebulous, or become concrete and pertinent to life, in proportion as it is illustrated by tangible experiences in his own life. The final objective of a liberal education, for example, is not learning what Plato meant by justice, but rather—utilizing Plato's definition and any other relevant ideas—determining what justice should mean today and learning how to make it a living reality. The student who appreciates and understands the world of living facts will comprehend ideas more solidly and vividly than the student who is naïve and inexperienced. He will have acquired a more comprehensive knowledge of the culture in which he lives and of the problems which confront society as it moves toward the better way of life. And there will be a greater likelihood that his intellectual grasp of these ideas will translate into action in his own further experience.

And if this argument is valid for the more abstract, philosophical concepts, it applies with full force to the subject matter of the various fields in which the student may major—chemistry, economics, journalism, sociology, physics, engineering.

The values, however, go beyond concreteness, and touch individual development in many other ways. Through off-campus experiences, especially when they are a directed part of the educational program, the student not only gains much broader conceptions of his human and physical environment, but learns of previously unknown opportunities through which he can explore for his own fuller development, and in which he may express himself in life; he makes observations of facts, verifies the validity of the classroom speculation, brings living problems back to the college laboratory;

and he acquires disciplined habits and skills which help make him personally and socially effective in his lifework. Or to state it another way, these experiences make valuable contributions to the classroom discussion, aid the student in finding and preparing himself vocationally, and help bring out his latent qualities of personality—his self-confidence and self-reliance, his initiative and ability to carry responsibility, his resourcefulness, and his effectiveness in personal and group activities.

These values, social and individual, deserve further elaboration. A principal objective of education is to have the student acquire a knowledge of the culture in which he lives. Now contemporary culture is something more than academic representations of it; it is a dynamic process, a synthesis of countless human relationships, a living reality. Descriptions are helpful in arousing expectations and in stimulating more precise and complete observations; and the interpretations of thoughtful and learned instructors are valuable in directing analysis and postulating further opinions. But a description is only a substitute for the real thing, and the interpretations lack validity to the individual until he has made them his own or rejected those which his own observation and experience do not bear out. In the process of examining existing culture, the class study and the supplementary experience go hand in hand.

Important in study is the accumulation of adequate and accurate observations and facts. Facts assembled by skilled observers are, of course, more reliable than those found through miscellaneous experience. But in a world given to errors, to mistaken judgments, and to the deliberate falsification and manufacture of information, there is required something more than acceptance of facts on the basis of authority. Intelligent action frequently requires the intuitive or common-sense verification of representations, a practice that is achieved through experience. And it is of equal importance to the thinking individual that he himself should fix in himself the habit of assembling reliable facts. This is the first requisite to independent thinking and acting.

Moreover, how effectively the individual learns to think depends in part on the intensity of his interest and his motivation. Interest and motivation are aroused when the student becomes aware of the significance of problems, actions, facts, and ideas. With awareness comes alertness. Alertness, as witness the Indian guide, is the result of sensitivity, which in turn has resulted from previous experience. The chain is endless, because an experience that makes a genuine impression on the person will arouse further interest. And as interest grows, there follows as a natural consequence greater motivation.

An essential step in thinking is to identify or define the problem or issue at stake; once this is done accurately and concisely, a problem is well on the way to solution. The quality needed is clearness of insight, discrimination in the choice of alternatives, penetration of analysis. This analytical ability again is coupled with sensitivity, alertness, awareness, which are achieved through the discipline of directed experience—experience in thinking, and experience in the verification of earlier deductions made or conclusions reached.

If we wish to apply this precise, discriminating kind of thinking to the facts and problems of present-day culture, we see that in so far as we can get personal experience to illuminate the complexities and the interplaying forces of that culture, such experience will best refine and sharpen the individual's own thinking. Getting this type of experience is in part a matter of bringing the student into stimulating contact with the more significant phases of, and facts about, life. More specifically, this means contact with the rural areas and the metropolitan centers; with the various classes of people—the laboring man, the white-collar worker, and the professional, social, or industrial leader; with industry, agriculture, service occupations, and institutions; with all sorts of human needs, conditions, and privileges. It means the observation of habits of life and social customs, and individual and group psychologies. It implies studying the aesthetics of practical affairs: seeing design in architecture and in economic activities; understanding the comeliness of eliminating waste, conserving resources, protecting health, educating people. It assumes the analytical observation of production and distribution, of power and facilities, and of the various forms of social organization. Such directed experience provides a basis for understanding the world of reality which both supplements and greatly enriches the understanding of the classroom.

In addition to increasing the individual's comprehension of the world about him and his power to be an effective force for the improvement of society, off-campus experience may contribute much to the student's personal development. First in importance is the finding of a vocational interest and securing some competence vocationally. Since the work in which a person engages occupies most of his productive time, provides his subsistence, and is the principal medium through which he makes his social contribution, it is fair to call selecting and preparing for this lifework a matter of primary concern to the individual. On the adjustment he is able to make to his vocation will depend most of his effectiveness in the work and much of his happiness in life.

Vocational adjustment involves several things: one is squaring the individual's vocational interest with his aptitudes. Enabling the individual to approach his fullest potentialities depends upon finding the most nearly appropriate interest—a process which unfortunately is far from simple. We do not yet have any one test by which aptitudes can be measured accurately. Instead, it is important to have the student analyze his own interests and abilities—an analysis that will be most fruitful if it is guided by a skilled counselor. Then there are personality inventory and general aptitude tests which the individual can take and which can also be interpreted by the counselor. And, of course, the subject matter which the individual studies with greatest success in the academic program provides clues. Orientation lectures can help to extend the horizons of his imagination. But whereas all these devices give indications of vocational aptitudes, only trial and error can confirm the tentative choices. Only actual experience can uncover unexpected sources of maladjustment, such as distaste for the sights or smells of the laboratory, nervous tensions under certain kinds of responsibilities, revulsion against the practices and customs of particular occupations. Varied experience, too, helps to uncover possible new choices, particularly if the counselor is directing the placement of the individual in line with his basic aptitudes. Finally, there is nothing like experience to arouse genuine interest.

A second factor in vocational adjustment is getting an

adequate foundation for one's chosen work. This involves, first of all, acquiring elementary skills fitting in with the tentative choice, which will serve as "ladder rungs" from which to make a successful start; next, it means obtaining the practical skills of action and of adjustment which can be obtained only while engaged in the work; and parallel to these, it includes more or less intensive study in the major field of concentration of which the vocation is a part.

The third aspect of vocational adjustment is the inter-relationship, which exists here as well as in the broader social problems, between theory and practice—as, for example, in chemistry. But the way experience can both stimulate and discipline the thinking has already been adequately presented.

A final factor of importance to a large number of individuals is early discovering congenial lifework and then immediately getting preparation for, and experience in, their chosen field. It seems only logical that, in so far as possible, the choice of the individual's major field should be consistent with his eventual lifework. Otherwise, there is much loss of time, effort, and interest on the part of the student, and partial waste of valuable human resources for society. It follows that the effort to find the student's functional work in society should be commenced early in the college career and carried forward as a continuing project until the adjust-ment seems to have been made. This procedure takes time from academic courses, but in the long run it is a great saver of time. In so far as it early incites the student to get inter-ested in his career, any time lost is quickly made up by the more intensive effort at learning he subsequently makes.

In addition to aiding greatly in vocational adjustment

off-campus experience helps the student improve his personal qualities in other ways, bringing out latent possibilities, and tempering and refining personality. Just "learning how to work" might pithily express this aim. And there is need for this learning since nearly half of the students coming to college in recent years have done almost no work—a lack which may presently have a decisive effect on our national character. But there is more to the idea of work than is at first apparent, for it involves not only becoming skilled and disciplined in physical effort, and learning how to use the hands in co-ordination with the brain; it includes also the developing of all those personal qualities which facilitate relationships with other people, and the expression of the individual's own objectives in a way that affects the lives of others.

Here, again, the first step is diagnosis under the direction of skilled counselors. This is not so much to uncover deficiencies as to stimulate the discovery and creation of new possibilities of growth. The discovery of special talents, such as manual dexterity, flair for design, or methodical habits, for example, contributes not only to vocational adjustment, but to the larger creative and productive possibilities of the individual as well. The verification of these talents is as likely to come from experience as from testing. There is also the question of spotting such characteristics as unusual diffidence, lack of self-confidence, awkwardness of human approaches, habits of slovenly appearance, or eccentric mannerisms, and shifting the student's environmental influence to give him the opportunity for improvement. Coupling the diagnosis with subsequent experience in an environment which dictates the change, also, aids greatly in making the student more acutely aware of the need for improvement, and in motivating him to try. A highly personal matter such as poor personal appearance can become, through experience in an actual situation, more impersonal; the counselor is thereby relieved of appearing impertinent and officious, and the student of his ordinarily defensive attitude.

Individuals need disciplining in skill and habit. Generally, work experience has a different tone, and makes different demands upon the individual from the usual demands of college. In work, for instance, there is the demand for clock-hour performance, necessitating habits of order and regularity, and for accuracy, skill, and quantity in results, which take attention and concentration. Responsibility in relationships to fellow workers is another valuable source of experience.

The assumption of responsibility implies a twofold relationship to others. One is responsiveness to the views and rights of other people; the second lies in what the individual must do to perform that responsibility. Again there are brought into play numerous possible personal qualities, such as sensitivity, alertness, self-assurance, and the habit of carrying thought into action, all of which give the student training both for leadership and for "followership."

There is a tendency for educated people to get further and further removed from the interests, needs, and aspirations of the common people. If democracy is to have genuine meaning, if the people as a whole are to have the full benefit of leadership from the educated members of society, there must be a continuing understanding and rapport between the college man and the persons who toil with their hands or till the earth. This can best be achieved by relating courses in such subjects as psychology, ethics, and philosophy to the students' experiences with people. For this reason all students might well have at least short-term experiences in factories, in department stores, on farms, and so forth. The experience of rubbing elbows with laborers in a factory or of taking case histories in a hospital, for example, helps the student to see that the mass of humanity is composed of individuals, and helps provide the common language and ideas important to good intercommunication. It also gives emotional warmth to the intellectual consideration of the vital problems in society.

For example, an Antioch student upon returning from a period of work in a federal employment bureau said that he had never before realized what unemployment meant in terms of human misery and social discontent. A few case histories had suddenly made the subject of economics vivid and vital for him. This experience, while he was still studying economic theory, helped greatly in preparing him for future leadership. Educated men cannot be effective leaders in a democracy until they have had emotional experiences like this.

As in seeking all objectives in education, different institutions will use different methods in this broader "experience-laboratory." The question is not one of adopting any one prescribed plan, but rather of finding some means of giving the student opportunities for experience which will bring the educational values desired. Various plans—like the co-operative plan of work and study originated at the University of Cincinnati and further developed at Antioch College and other institutions, of the plan of a midwinter period of experience used at Bennington and Bard colleges, of the plan of a semester or summer's experience used by a few institutions—have been tried with considerable success. The work of many instructors in requiring community or special surveys as a part of particular courses of study, and of other instructors in encouraging students to participate in political and civic activities, is well known. Since more reliable information about these plans can be secured directly from the respective institutions, their individual merits will not be examined here.

The world is, of course, at the elbow of the institution, waiting to be observed. It is, further, a natural expectation on the part of young people that they shall have experience in it. To an important extent, students are already gaining experience in it, but since the experience is undirected much of its potential value is lost. Naturally, a specific plan of combining practical work with study involves both careful planning on the part of the institution and extensive co-operation from outside employers. That this co-operation can be secured is evident from the success of the institutions which have sought it. The advantages are not all with the student. The social advantages, such as that of providing a new type and capacity of leadership, accrue in part to the participating employer. Indeed, if the work-and-study plan were much more widely adopted, with the ultimate effect of providing an ample supply of potential leaders having this education, individual firms would benefit considerably thereby. And if we assume adequate care in the placement on jobs, there is ordinarily no question of any employer's getting immediate and specific returns now for his expenditure of time and funds. Students try hard to succeed in their positions, and put more than average energy and intelligence into the attempt.

The planning required on the part of the college includes devising means of directing the experiences of the students along educational lines, and of analyzing the meaning of the experiences. For both purposes it is important to define the objectives. These are, as indicated, both personal and social. If the planning is to reach the individual's needs, such as exploring for vocational interest and aptitude, it must be individualized. Close co-operation between the student and the counselor is needed to work out a sequence of experiences which will get the desired educational result—finding the right vocation, acquiring skills in social relationships, supplementing and expanding the student's knowledge and competence in a particular field, and so forth. The co-operation of the instructors in particular courses is also needed in order that the student of labor relations, of chemistry, or of public administration may get the maximum values from his off-campus experiences.

The planning required to get from experience the desired social values—the values which should emerge as part of the liberal education of the student—may be done either in terms of groups, or of the time and content sequences of the curriculum. Obviously, the off-campus experience should be an integral part of the study of the broad social problems recommended in Chapter VI. Or, if the college handles this part of the program through survey courses, the experiences and observations in the field should be interrelated with the classroom work on the campus. Probably the best method is to work out syllabi for the study of particular problems, including in the syllabus directions for off-campus observations and experiences, and directions for the preparation of a thesis upon the subject. These ideas can be worked into a single pattern. For example, a broad survey course in economic and social problems can, utilizing the syllabus-thesis technique, carry right through both the study and work periods (assuming they alternate), thus both directing the experiences and interpreting their meaning. Or the general reading program, suggested in Chapter VII, can be co-ordinated with the planned activities of the experience periods. If this reading and writing program were also utilized as the medium for gaining facility in verbalization and expertness in composition, the results would probably be better and more lasting than the results often secured from the typical Freshman English course.

An advantage of the "experience-laboratory" lies in its individualized approach. Particularly when the work placement plan is used, the individual student must be considered upon the basis of his own particular needs and merits, and the responsibilities which he assumes must of necessity be individual to him. Coupled with a sound counseling system, this breaking away from the mass system in education has obvious advantages. Especially marked is the growth of personal maturity, which is one important phase of personal development.

CHAPTER XIII

THE INSTRUCTOR AS EDUCATOR

CENTRAL to the program suggested in this book is the place and function of the teacher. Teaching has been defined as the stimulation, counseling, and instruction of the student, a phrase used pointedly, to convey a larger conception of the teaching function than that often held by college teachers. The instructor should be an educator of students, and not primarily a teacher of subjects. Courses of instruction provide the meat of the curriculum; they should be substantial in content and thorough in requirements; but they are the means to the end of educating students, not the end itself. To put too much emphasis upon them lets them dominate the thinking of the faculty. Frequently the man whose interest lies in research fails as a teacher because the details of his subject matter continue to dominate his thinking even after he has lost the interest of his students. Actually the courses of study need much supplementation and implementation in order to be effective as educational devices. And the individual student is the objective toward which the whole educational effort is directed.

The terms "stimulate," "counsel," and "instruct" need more specific definition. They are not narrow, nor are they mutually exclusive. They are designed here to be cumulative in effect—progressive in their scope in the order given.

By stimulation is meant the arousing of the students' interest, engaging their intelligence in activity, encouraging them to make trials as part of the trial-and-error process of experimentation. Stimulating the student is not best accomplished by overwhelming him with such effulgence of personality as the instructor can command. Personal qualities of sympathy, earnestness, and objectivity are, of course, essential to the counselor. But stimulating educationally implies the careful and systematic study of the student, utilizing the information about him provided by the records of the college, and the observations derived through conferences and otherwise, in an effort to understand him as thoroughly as possible, to discover his potentialities for development, and then to aid him in finding points of intellectual interest from which to make departures for further learning. The intuitive flashes of insight which the observer of the student will occasionally get are valuable, but these flashes will come as the result either of knowing the student well or of having had considerable experience in carefully analyzing personalities.

Stimulation, also, does not come solely through counseling contacts. Every experience the student has may conceivably contribute to this end. For instance, the instructor may be so enthusiastic about his subject matter that he attracts the full attention and interest of the student. And a reason for establishing a wider and richer environment in which the student may gain experience is to catch and fire his imagination. But the instructor plays an essential role in interpreting these experiences, in an effort to relate the student's potential interests to his apparent talents.

The counseling of students is a broader matter than stimulation, since the stimulation is only one step in guidance. Interest and activity, once aroused, must be pointed in some direction. To counsel the student is to assist him to determine possible courses of action, and to decide upon the one among the various alternatives which will be best for him. An essential is, of course, to help define the criteria the student will use in making the decision.

One important distinction to make is between the *function* of counseling and particular *systems* of counseling. The latter may be either broad or extremely narrow. The function of counseling, however, is part of the teaching function, and not merely part of the mechanics of registration. It is an aid to the student in finding his way, in thinking out his life's philosophy and courses of action.

Instruction is a still broader term. Through instruction, the teacher aids the student in coming to understand problems and materials, and in gaining competence in attacking, analyzing, and synthesizing these problems and materials. Instruction includes the exposition of subject matter; but it is something more. Just as a student does not learn to play the violin until he has made at least some of the knowledge of the instructor his own, so the individual does not become educated in any field until he has converted the knowledge possessed by others into bases for action in his own life.

Also, instruction should not be confined to the classroom, but should be the basis for the counseling program and should permeate the whole of the activities of the institution. Consistent with the ideal of developing the whole personality of the individual is the concept of taking the opportunity for instructing him in all phases of his development. The teaching opportunity which normally exists in incidents and problems which arise in campus life, or in the off-campus experiences, has been noted. If instruction is to be most effective, the individual must be distinguished from the mass, and the instruction must reach him in terms significant to him in his own life. At the same time, since one of the objectives is to learn how to derive the highest advantages from group living and endeavor, leadership is necessary in thinking and acting with groups of individuals.

The members of the faculty who direct extraclass activities should especially be encouraged to emphasize the educational values in their work. The dramatics coach, the orchestra leaders, and the athletics instructor, for instance, should be judged for advancement not on their showmanship and "results," but on their abilities as educators in stimulating general participation in these activities, and in developing the creative faculties of the students who have potential abilities in these directions.

A moment's reflection will show that the best results require considerable diversity of methods in teaching, or really a combination of several methods. The tutorial method reaches the individual student and stimulates him to his best endeavor. In part also, however, the usual methods of lecturing, class discussions, laboratory experimentation, motion pictures, field trips, and so forth may be used and have their place. To some extent the instructor should be free to utilize those methods which are best adapted to his subject or objectives, and which he finds to be most effective—but his effectiveness with his chosen methods should be checked occasionally, in co-operation with the administration, and changed when the need is evident.

Teaching is both a science and an art. It is a science in

that careful planning of objectives, methods, content, and measures of results or achievement is required of the instructor; it is also an art because the teacher needs qualities such as sensitivity to the progress of the student, sympathetic personal relationships, and skill in working with the individual. Teaching is one of the finer of the arts; it is in fact surprising that more teachers do not make greater effort to improve their skill, and take greater professional pride in producing masters among their students.

Teaching also has ethical implications. It is sometimes contended by members of the faculty that their responsibility to the educational institution is confined to the hours during which direct service is being rendered. Proposed codes of academic freedom sometimes include the provision that the faculty may live their own lives as they please when off duty. Obviously there is need for common understanding on this point because an instructor cannot be expected to work during any and all hours of the day and night, nor should he be subjected to rules and regulations concerning his mode of life—regulations which sometimes take exceedingly petty forms. But the innuendo which can be read into these codes is that the private or off-campus life of the instructor is no concern of the institution—which is, in this analysis of the function of liberal education, an egregious error. There is no more logic in having a code to protect the instructor in this area than in a code to restrict him.

What is needed within the staff of the institution is unity of purpose. In the larger sense, the aim of teaching is the achievement of an ethical objective: the search for the best way of life. (It should be evident by this time that this phrase does not refer to mid-Victorian morals.) To pursue this goal with sincerity of purpose and scholarly methods is a responsibility of every member of the faculty. To have any meaning at all, his classroom enunciations must be consistent with his own mode of living, and vice versa.

The relationship of teaching to the administration of the college has also been noted. Logically, it would seem that the colleges, of all organized social groups, should have need for the fewest rules and regulations governing the actions of their members, faculty or students. No more idealistic or homogeneous groups could well be found. Actually, institutions tend to be cluttered up with regulations, the motive behind which may be lofty. But the imposition of authority from above simply displaces thinking. Now, it is the instructor's job to stimulate and direct thinking. The greatest administrative efficiency arises as a by-product of the greatest educational efficiency: the educational approach to campus living economizes greatly on administration because it gets at the causes of problems.

This exposition of the teaching function has implications in the selection and training of college teachers. It indicates, for instance, that the knowledge of a special field should not be the whole or even the controlling factor in selecting instructors for the college of liberal arts. Thorough preparation in a field is essential; but emphasis on that preparation must not obscure the importance of much broader training and outlook on life if the individual is to meet adequately the requirements of the teaching function. Certain personal qualifications are essential, such as the ability to express oneself clearly in writing or speaking, or to work with young people sympathetically and earnestly. And the adaptability or versatility of the prospective teacher in applying his skills in thinking and his knowledge to the broader problems of society is important. Furthermore, the breadth of interest and the kind of motivation possessed by the individual are significant, if the objective of the liberal college is not to be undermined or at best left unsupported.

In preparing college teachers, the graduate schools do not do the whole of the job that is needed. What they do do is excellent and vital; but in their extreme emphasis upon specialized study, they tend to leave untouched other matters. Especially should the search for higher values be continued and intensified, thus introducing a broad philosophical element into the content of the graduate curriculum. The graduate schools overlook an important educational principle —that the development of the qualities required for teaching does not take place in one direction at a time; such development means simultaneous growth in all the directions which vitalize the creative personality. In the graduate school, as elsewhere, attention to these matters not only would not interfere with, but would enhance, intellectual growth.

To the extent that new members of the faculty are uninterested or unskilled in the larger teaching function, it is wise for the institution to organize some means of stimulating their interest and of training them. Ordinarily this is not a large task, for the young person entering upon the profession of a lifetime can readily see the larger aspects of that profession once they are pointed out to him. A program for these newer faculty should be organized in any event, to acquaint them with the particular aims and methods of the institution, or to provide a contact through which their progress in their work can be observed. For young instructors need to be instructed, and not merely left to sink or swim; also, they need to be sorted out with care in the first years of their effort.

The fulfilling of the teaching function is the immediate responsibility of the instructor. But beyond this, there is the larger one of living. Not as example, but by way of leadership, the college instructor should occupy a niche of significance in society, and be a creative factor in working for a better way of life. As one thoughtful educator, Alexander Meiklejohn, asked: "How can it be brought about that the teachers in our colleges and universities shall see themselves, not only as the servants of scholarship, but also, in a far deeper sense, as the creators of the national intelligence?"[1]

[1] Alexander Meiklejohn, *The Experimental College*, p. 317. New York: Harper & Brothers, 1932.

CHAPTER XIV

THE STUDENT BEFORE AND AFTER

WHILE the high schools have been expanding their curricula in various new directions, the college professors have been beating their breasts at the lack of student preparation for college-grade work. They may as well relax. The trend will not be reversed. For the high schools are discovering that they have a broader function than just preparing students for college. They are discovering that education, at all levels, is a means of learning how to live a fuller and more successful life. And attention to the new discovery is causing them to neglect some of the elements which have traditionally been considered important in the preparation for college.

Students of college caliber should be much better prepared for intellectual work than they are, but this is a fault of our mass system of education rather than of specific curricula. Students having intellectual talents should receive greater individual attention in such basic matters as learning to read with comprehension and to write with ease and skill. They are not likely to get it until the schools of the country are more adequately staffed both in numbers and in professional qualifications than they are at present.

The high-school curriculum, in substantial part, has been expanded in directions little understood by the colleges. It includes "social living," and "life sciences," and "economic life," and "home art," and what not. These courses are for the most part a step in the right direction. They are experimental, and have weaknesses characteristic of new methods, but they are sound in their aim as a whole. The same can be said for the elementary schools; and the nursery schools, starting as they have without binding traditions, have done the best job of all in devising excellent new methods of instruction. But it is not a part of the function of this book to examine these developments, or to appraise them. It suffices to note their existence.

The educational trends on the secondary level for the near future are probably foreshadowed in this report of the American Youth Commission:

Because of the changing composition of the high school population, the situation has become so acute during the last ten years that it has become obvious that fundamental reorganization of the secondary school curriculum can no longer be deferred. After several extensive surveys of the problem had been made by various organizations, it appeared that some agreement on major lines of reorganization might be possible. Under the auspices of this Commission, a special committee was called together and the result was the brief report entitled *What the High Schools Ought to Teach*, published in August, 1940, with the commendation and approval of this Commission.

In that report the initial emphasis was given to the importance of continued instruction in reading as an important and much neglected element in the high school curriculum. Equal emphasis was given to work as a factor in general education second in importance to none. Instruction in the social studies and instruction to prepare young people to meet major personal problems were stressed as essential elements of the reorganized curriculum. The traditional course of study, particularly in the ninth grade, was attacked as inappropriate for many young people, as destructive of pupil interest, and as standing in the way of the curriculum reconstruction which in some manner must take place.[1]

It is interesting to compare the recommendations made here for the secondary curriculum with those made earlier in this book concerning the course, reading, problems, and experience phases of the program on the college level.

The existence of these trends carries implications for the college. One is that the college can no longer expect uniform preparation in specific subject matter on the part of the secondary-school graduate. This necessitates a new kind of co-ordination between high school and college. Formerly the co-ordination was largely a certain standard sequence in the subject matter of the freshman year, which presumably carried on from the sequence of the preparatory or high school. The emphasis all the way along was on course sequences. This is much less possible today. The test of admission to college can hardly continue to be the successful completion of certain specific courses; the new co-ordination must take into consideration the stage of personal development, the quality of living, achieved by the student. This is a much more difficult thing to measure, and there is no longer, as formerly, one easy test. A variety of tests must be used, including the new types of tests for aptitudes, achievement, and personal growth.

The aptitude tests indicate the presence (or lack of it) of adequate intelligence and general native ability. The achievement examinations can be constructed for the purposes of the particular institution, but should always reveal

[1] American Council on Education, General Report of the American Youth Commission, *Youth and the Future*, p. 117. Washington, 1942.

the general knowledge in any one area that the student has acquired by the time he enters college. Broken down, the results from these tests will also serve as a basis for guiding the student in his first course selections in college.

Another implication for the college is that more individualization is now required. It is of particular importance, using the achievement results just noted, to help the student fill in holes in his background—in areas like mathematics or chemistry, for instance, where he may not have the necessary training to do the college work. These holes are not a cause for major concern, for given the intelligence which the student should possess to warrant admission to the liberal curriculum, the time required to make up these deficiencies is negligible. But it does require devoting some teaching effort to individualized clinics.

The opposite of deficiencies is unusual achievement. There is no justification for the duplication of secondary-school work frequently required of freshmen in college. Achievement should be recognized and the student permitted to pass on into higher course levels. Far from showing sad preparation for college, the tests frequently demonstrate that a student is not only at college level but, in particular areas, well along.[2]

A final use of the new criteria for admission to college is to break away from the rigid requirement of high-school graduation. When an individual who for some reason has failed to attend high school, or to graduate from one, later determines to get a formal college education, he should be

[2] See, for example, the case histories described in *An Experiment in Responsible Learning*, Bulletin No. 31, The Carnegie Foundation for the Advancement of Teaching, New York, 1940.

given the opportunity if he possesses the requisite aptitudes and general achievement. The new methods of measuring aptitudes and achievement are a reasonably satisfactory basis for determining whether he should be given the chance. This is not a suggestion that the colleges invade the junior or senior years of the high school—as is apt to be the temptation under the pressure of wartime conditions. It is instead a plea for the recognition of achievement rather than timeserving as the basis for advancement.

This chapter deals with the individual before and after college. Not all students graduate. In fact, a substantial portion of the "after" group are those who have dropped out by the way. These students deserve more consideration than they commonly get.

There is, of course, the much-debated point whether the college program should be designed on the assumption that all students will graduate, or whether it should provide the student with an education of value in life at whatever point he departs from the institution. Some would contend that these two ideas are not inconsistent, that the typical sequential program is the best one either way. Others argue the same view, but on the assumption that the best program is the one which continuously teaches the student the art of better living.

The important thing is to relate the education of the individual to his own planning for his future, whatever it may be at the moment. Thus, if the student knows that he is going through to graduation, or fully expects to go on to graduate or professional school, he should plan his program accordingly. A student committed to the study of medicine, for example, has definite requirements for his undergraduate program. If, on the other hand, he is uncertain about the length of his education but has other fairly definite aims in view, he should plan in the direction indicated by those aims. It is always valuable to have a goal ahead, even though the chance is considerable that the goal will be changed or enlarged as time goes on. And the college program should be sufficiently flexible to enable the individual to get a program consistent with his own plans. This does not mean elaborate curricula; it does mean keeping the way open throughout the program for individual variations. It means, for instance, permitting the student to take at least some work in the field of particular interest to him at any given time, freshman year or otherwise.

Incidentally, this flexibility in curriculum, combined with the experience provided by off-campus work, gives a basis for making adjustments in individual cases. Too often the student who fails to make a good start in the general program is dismissed as a failure. This is a negative action, harmful both to the student and to the institution. The more flexible and varied program enables the college to prepare the individual for effort along lines more suited to his abilities or interests than academic study may be, and to steer him into them in a more constructive way.

An important aim of the college work is to prepare for graduate or professional study. There is nothing inconsistent in this aim with the general program proposed. Primary objectives have been to increase the individual's power to think effectively, to broaden his acquaintance with vital social issues, and to give him some proficiency in a field of special interest, all of which fit in with the idea of further study. Indeed, if the student's appetite for knowledge has been at all stimulated, further formalized study would be the natural course for many.

Incidentally, better co-ordination in purpose is needed at this point, too. Much professionalized work, now given on the undergraduate level, should be pushed on to the higher levels. Giving the student more time for cultural subjects would provide society with better business leaders, teachers, and engineers. And the professional and graduate schools should enable the individual to continue his general development. If the law and medical schools, for example, gave more study to social philosophy, the practitioners in these professions might possess a more discriminating social-mindedness than on the average they now do.

The principle, preparing for life by learning to live fully, has a bearing upon alumni relations generally. The effort of the college is in part wasted if the graduates fail to carry on in this spirit after being graduated; the college will have been at some fault here for not knowing how to reach these individuals effectively, or for having been careless in its efforts to aid them in planning and working toward this end. The interweaving of study with work aids greatly in securing a carry-over from college to postcollege life. But with the best of planning and effort, some graduates will fail to take hold or to live up to the expectations the college had of them. Here the college can, perhaps, conserve a portion of its social investment if it will follow these individuals a little further with stimulation and guidance.

Then, too, the alumni could well continue in several kinds of group relationship with the institution. If the function of a liberal education is aiding society in the solution of its essential problems and in progressing to a higher level of culture, this function must find expression in the lives of the graduates of the college. In view of the common purpose, the alumni could add strength to the college group, as well as provide it with additional leadership, if they would join in particular group endeavors. An active group interested in planning a better world order, for instance, composed of alumni, faculty, and students, would possess considerable strength.

It is not strictly within the scope of this volume, but it may help in showing the relationships suggested in this chapter if a brief picture is given of the kind of educational program that is suitable and essential to a democracy. The principle of freeing the individual to develop in line with his personal potentialities requires greatly varied educational opportunities. It assumes a further development of the science of discovering individual aptitudes and talents. It implies the recognition that a talent such as finger dexterity, or sensitivity to color harmony, or unusual muscular coordination has its place in a democratic society just as much as a high intellectual quotient or political suavity. And since education is the best medium through which growth of all types can be stimulated and cultivated, facilities must be provided which will permit the individual to continue his development as long as his growth warrants the social expenditure.

Of particular importance to society, however, is the keeping alive and active such intellectual acumen as the individual may have. The present educational system with its preponderance of discrete courses, its emphasis on grades and credits, and its assumption that an education is something tangible—a distinct body of knowledge given by the school to the pupil—tends to defeat this purpose. Intellectual curiosity is blunted instead of being whetted. The critical approach is converted into the conformist attitude. Knowledge is presented as the final word rather than as a growing process. The student gets his diploma, and his education stops. Is it naïve to feel that this should not be true of even the average high-school graduate? And if democracy is to be a genuine success, it must encourage critical thinking and active experimental study about its problems. This applies not alone to its leaders; it is important for the general run of its citizens, also.

Here we get down to a bedrock assumption of this book—that the great mass of the people are educable. There are evident too many farmers with only elementary-school education, for instance, who possess substantial knowledge of farming and keenly discriminating judgment in it and who use the experimental method in improving the products of their work, to permit one to believe that there does not exist among the common people large capacity for growth. Of course, one's belief depends in part upon how he defines "educable." But the opposite theory—that only a few have capacity—is harmful, like the older English theory, for instance, that to educate the children of the working class beyond the age of fifteen merely makes them maladjusted and less happy in life. We don't yet know enough about the learning process to be sure of any such theories. Recent studies, for example, indicate that we shall have to revise our notions about the fixity of the I. Q.

The educational program should more nearly resemble a telescope than a stack of concrete blocks. Education should start with the individual where he is and expand, in ever-widening horizons. At the same time it should provide intensity of experience, which leads always forward to as yet unexplored (for the individual) knowledge. Many of a person's basic characteristics, both individual and social, are fixed in his earliest years—hence the importance of having an adequate nursery-school program to supplement (and often reform) the home influence. As the child ascends in the educational scale, each new phase of the program should provide a broader and deeper experience. In music, for instance, appreciation is not learned in a single course; it comes through a combination of courses which broaden one's concept of music, together with continuous opportunity to hear and participate in good music. Is not the same thing true for sensitivity to beauty, for curiosity about facts, for discrimination of judgment concerning social and antisocial, for the ability to solve problems in some field? Psychologists are not sure that there is any limit to this growth. The moral is that the educational system should provide a continuing stimulation over the years, and opportunities for education in line with the individual's growing capacities and his particular aptitudes. Logically, this should be continued into the field of adult education, which has possibilities for development as yet untouched. As with the telescope, there should always appear to be something more just beyond the limits of our present powers of vision.

CHAPTER XV

THE PROGRAM AS A WHOLE: RECAPITULATION

AT THE risk of repetition, the principal ideas outlined thus far will now be summarized briefly to show them in relation to each other and as a whole. The ideas, primarily, concern the purpose, content, and method of the college program, the function of the faculty, and the method of organizing to achieve the objectives.

These ideas entail certain basic assumptions: that a more perfect society than the present one can be attained; that its characteristics are not fully disclosed in some predetermined pattern, but must be discovered experimentally; that man is able to plan ahead at successive steps in helping determine what human progress shall be; and that the direction lies in searching for the greatest possible development of the potentialities of the individual personality consistent with securing the maximum benefits to be derived from group association and endeavor.

Each individual is a distinctive personality, with interests and talents peculiar to himself. In the ideal society, he should be free to develop himself vocationally and avocationally, in personal and social effectiveness, in his acquaintance with his physical and human environment, and in a growing philosophy of life. Although the ideal society must be discovered experimentally, the meditations of the philosophers and the experience of history suggest in general terms the courses of action through which to achieve the maximum benefits of group living. These can best be seen as contrasts: the co-operative way rather than the way of strife; the way of tolerance, good will, and mutual recognition of rights rather than of intolerance, hate, and suppression; the way of determining action by common consent and fulfilling it through voluntary participation, rather than by regimentation and the pushing of others around.

The route to attaining these objectives is to apply the intelligence toward learning how to live more fully, both individually and from the social viewpoint. The function of a liberal education is to assist in this process; the function of the liberal college is therefore tied to broad social purposes. Its endeavor always is to distill other human experience, past and contemporary, for the light it will shed upon the good way of life. The principal medium for the diffusion in society of these results lies in the students who come to be educated.

The development that is possible for the individual has been suggested both generally and in detail. A broad view of the subject has been taken because attention to such matters as health, vocational adjustment, and refinement of social attitudes not only does not detract from, but actually enhances, the intellectual advancement. This is because the arousing of interest and the development of personal and social effectiveness are a part both of intellectual stimulation and of making thought effective in action. But a primary aim of the liberal college must always be that of developing the power to think—which in itself assumes the proper function of knowledge, the use of the scientific method, and learning to apply thinking to the practical problems of life. Above all must come a maturing philosophy of life, in itself the result of thinking, which progressively sets the direction of growth both for the personal life of the individual and for the endeavor to secure higher social values.

The college fulfills its function by organizing a program. It is suggested that the focal point for this program lies in the vital problems of present-day society, since finding a better way of life is first of all a matter of solving these problems. The solution of one problem always creates new problems; but the problems are points of attack, and each effort at definition and solution tends to raise the general level of culture.

The students start then with the same challenge which has always in society confronted the intelligent leaders in thought and action—that of realizing a better life on earth. The general problems, of necessity, lead to the more specialized study of particular ones. These particular problems will be both those which have arisen out of the personal experience or immediate environment of the student, and those which confront him and attract his interest as a result of the educational program. Part of the procedure is to plan a group of problems which will best meet these objectives, and part is to place the student in a gradually more stimulating environment through which he will observe and meet new problems, some of which will become important to him.

The basis for the program, therefore, is an environment for the student which has been planned to be as effective as possible in stimulating, guiding, and instructing him. This means working with the student in his total environment.

The provision of appropriate curricula is emphasized, and attention is given to methods of counseling and instruction. But use is also made of the normal life of the college community for experimentation in democratic methods and improved ways of living, for developing more substantial activities and more refined avocational and other interests, and for securing greater discrimination concerning values. Further, there is experience in off-campus activities— again to help the student determine upon interests, adjust vocationally, develop personal and social effectiveness in many ways—and above all to help him gain a more comprehensive and accurate knowledge of the world in which we live, acquire a sensitivity to the needs and aspirations of the people who do physical labor and learn how to speak their language, observe facts and test ideas in experience, and generally temper and sharpen his judgment. The program functions as a unit, the study of problems, facts, and principles in the classroom stimulating interest in outside activity and giving a basis for richer and more educational experience; and the activities on and off the campus both testing the classroom theories in practice and providing fresh attitudes, approaches, materials, and problems for further work in the courses of study.

Although the approach to study is through problems important to society and significant to the student, and there is a corresponding emphasis upon studying and improving contemporary culture, the cultural heritage of the past is not neglected. The present has grown out of the past, and study of the past is necessary if we are to gain perspective on trends and values, and to secure and appraise the accumulated wisdom and material savings from past generations.

Except for the individual who makes it a field of specialized study, however, the past is not studied as an end in itself, but in relation to the present. It is drawn upon to throw light upon the facts and problems of the present, to indicate values and goals which are most worth striving for today, and to give us greater enjoyment while living in the present.

To correct the provincialism in outlook which prevails in the American college, it is suggested that other cultures contemporary with our own be studied. The age of science is having a profound effect in advancing the modes of living of other national and racial groups. We shall be shortsighted if we do not make use of the wisdom of other cultural groups to complement that which arises from our own history.

Education is growth in the direction of living more fully. Growth takes place both extensively and intensively. The program, therefore, should induce growth concurrently both in broader directions and in more intensive ways. Emphasis on both aspects of growth is continuous throughout the program. The general and the special, the cultural and the vocational, the theoretical and the practical applications are carried simultaneously.

Growth should also be continuous in time if the highest potentialities for the individual are to be realized. Emphasis is therefore placed upon several lines of continuity which run throughout the years at college, partly to secure this continuing development, and partly to establish them as habits in the individual even after he has finished his education. There is the study of vital social problems, continued every year; the acquisition of competence in a field of academic concentration, which the student may begin even in his freshman year; the continuous exposure to an increasingly stimulating environment, and the interweaving of normal life experiences with the academic study; the regular preparation of major written reports, the continuous resort to the methods of the laboratory, and the reading program which proceeds steadily through the college years; there is the constant endeavor to individualize the program, to make it sufficiently flexible to meet the student's needs, to induce the habit of self-education, and to help the individual develop integrity and responsibility through assuming responsibilities in line with his capacities. There is, finally, a consistent use of the democratic method in organization and educational functioning.

There is still another major thread of continuity. Teachers are cautioned to be teachers of students first, and of subject matter as the means toward this end. The arousing of interest and the development of personal and social effectiveness are a part both of intellectual stimulation and of making thought effective in action. But a primary aim of the liberal college must always be that of developing the power to think—which in itself assumes the proper function of knowledge, the use of the scientific method, and learning to apply thinking to the practical problems of life. Above all must come a maturing philosophy of life, in itself the result of thinking, which progressively sets the direction of growth both for the personal life of the individual and for the endeavor to secure higher social values.

The college fulfills its function by organizing a program. It is suggested that the focal point for this program lies in the vital problems of present-day society, since finding a better way of life is first of all a matter of solving these problems. The solution of one problem always creates new problems. The problems are thus points of attack, and each effort at definition and solution tends to raise the general level of culture.

The students start, then, with the same challenge which has always in society confronted the intelligent leaders in thought and action—that of realizing a better life on earth. The general problems, of necessity, lead to the more specialized study of particular ones. These particular problems will be both those which have arisen out of the personal experience or immediate environment of the students and those which confront him and attract his interest as a result of the educational program. Part of the teaching function is the broad one of stimulating, counseling, and instructing the student, both concerning the whole of his personal development and concerning his functions as a social being. The instructor, therefore, is the key person around whom the various elements of the program revolve. To be effective, he must himself have the qualities of interest and enthusiasm, breadth of outlook, intellectual competence, active participation in socially valuable activities, and the ability to live a full life. To secure the desired educational result he must stimulate the student to educate himself. And as a first step, he must know the student, and know him well.

The goal of this educational program is progress in growth. The direction is toward the more perfect society. Growth of the student, in his sensitivity to human values, in his understanding of vital issues, and in his effectiveness for productive effort, personally and in his capacity for social leadership, is a primary requisite for progress in this direction. The program suggested, however, need not be as ponderously serious as all this may sound. For a primary objective always is to teach the student the art of living. And a full life includes fun and recreation, hobbies and avocational endeavor, as well as serious study, research, and work.

CHAPTER XVI

EDUCATION FOR WHAT?

THERE should be an ethical aim in education. This is because it is the means of directing men's intelligence toward larger objectives than those individual men might hit on in a primitive society—objectives which mean greater accomplishment for the group and thus have profound bearings upon men's lives. The effects of educating German youth in the deliberately framed doctrines of Nazi ideology furnish us with an immediate example of the importance of defining the ethical aims.

Some perspective concerning aims is gained from noting the educational emphases or aims in particular periods in history or those advocated by influential philosophers. Some of these aims have been narrowly conceived, whereas others are broad in their ethical concepts. Examples of narrowness in conception are: the Spartan emphasis on military proficiency; medieval emphasis on courtliness; later humanistic emphasis on Latin style; American colonial emphasis on theology; Prussian emphasis on regimentation and obedience; French emphasis on intellectualism; English emphasis on Greek and Latin and sports; and current German emphasis on racism.

Examples of a broader conception of purposes in education are: the Athenian aim of individual excellence for state usefulness; Plato's aim of virtue in the individual and justice in the state; Aristotle's aim of well-being and well-doing through development of man's threefold nature; the early Roman aim of the *vir bonus*; Milton's aim to fit a man to perform justly, skillfully, and magnanimously all the offices both private and public of both peace and war; Locke's aim of virtue, worldly wisdom, learning; Pestalozzi's aim of the natural progressive and harmonious development of the powers and capacities of the human being; Froebel's aim of developing the latent powers of the individual, to exalt them into "a life of creative freedom";[1] Spencer's aim of preparation for complete living; Dewey's aim of utilizing experience as an educational method in enriching the whole of the living of the individual.

Looked at in the perspective of history, the inadequacy—and occasionally the viciousness—of the narrow approach to the definition of ethical aims is evident. For example, the medieval emphasis on courtliness is now amusing, the Nazi emphasis on racism is tragic. The goals sought by those who stated their objectives in a more inclusive way, however, all have something in common. This is the direction of their ethical thinking. The persons involved were searching for the good life, through perfecting either the individual or the state, or both.

The preceding chapters have related the educational purpose and effort to the ideal goal stated in this general formula: The objective of society should be to enable each individual to achieve the fullest development of his own personality and life consistent with, and at the same time

[1] Friedrich Froebel, *The Education of Man*, p. 332. New York: D. Appleton and Company, 1887.

capturing for society as a whole, the maximum values which can be gained from group association and endeavor. This ethical purpose seems in general to be harmonious with the aims of those philosophers of the past and present who have not been content with considering anything less than the whole of the individual and the whole of humanity in planning methods. Such a goal tends to be universal in application.

But this goal is also abstract. For the individual, the institution, and society, it needs more concrete definition. Without departing from over-all ideals, or consistent research to find better ways of living in harmony with them, the institution and its faculty need to apply them in everyday life to concrete situations. Otherwise education has little genuine significance.

The liberal arts college has to be something more than a repository of knowledge, presenting all sides of every problem, and remaining neutral in all controversies. This attitude is all too common among college faculties. Its causes may lie in a mistaken notion of what scholarship means, or in the doubtful belief that the instructor should lean over backward lest he influence the opinions of his students, or possibly in sheer timidity born of the lack of experience in the realistic world. Whatever the causes, it is doubtful if this educational policy can serve the true function of the liberal college.

With this point of view many educators are coming to agree. Some express their convictions in religious (as does Cole, for example) and others in metaphysical terms. The viewpoint is essentially that held by Christian Gauss:

Higher education must consider whether the most serious single cause for the weakening of the liberal tradition does not lie precisely in the fact that humanists and historians, cowed by the success of scientists, have developed an inferiority complex and have become afraid to pronounce moral and esthetic judgments. They have forgotten that the liberal tradition rested upon moral principles which it was their particular duty to defend. The pretensions of the newer, anarchical, totalitarian or nationalistic states can be curbed only if we reaffirm those principles . . . If the humanist has a function it is to evaluate and tell us what elements in life, what creations in art, are worth while, have a bearing upon the welfare of man. This means *passing judgments*, an art the humanist has forgotten.[2]

If it is to do its social job today, the college, meaning the persons of which it is composed, almost has to be motivated strongly toward some such ideal as the one here propounded, and should take positions of leadership and influence in an effort to bring the ideal to fuller realization in society. Provided they maintain tolerance and freedom for individuals who disagree (for otherwise the policy would become dogmatic), the majority of the faculty has the right and the responsibility to set an institutional direction and to assert leadership in specific ways. Certainly the individual instructors have that right and responsibility for themselves. For to produce effective and vital leaders for our dynamic society —artists, scientists, social engineers, administrators, and statesmen, philosophers all—the faculty should be examples in vision, courage, and social effort.

In this process—essentially a research one, both for the individual and for the institution—there exist the means of reappraising and defining values as civilization moves forward. If truth is relative, the best approaches to it lie in the diversified studies of many thousands of scholars and insti-

[2] Christian Gauss, "Can We Educate for Democracy?" *American Scholar*, Summer, 1942, pp. 370, 371.

tutions. The heart of the studies is to find those modes of living which give continuity to a culture, and which in the trial-and-error process of living have been found to have survival value and social utility. From the cumulative effect of this research there can be skimmed off a residue of principles which become the basic truths by which to live for the present and the near future.

There are countless avenues of effort. The scientist can continue to help solve the mysteries of the universe and apply the results to some social purpose—for instance, we know almost nothing about how the green plant, utilizing sunlight, stores up food and solid matter for future human use. The artist can bring beauty into everyday life. The social engineer can help in gaining a more equitable distribution of the essentials of life, in eliminating the causes of poverty, insecurity, illness, and war, and in providing better education. The administrator and the statesman in their respective spheres can aid in devising forms and methods of social organization to achieve these ends. As philosophers, they all can pose hypotheses of human behavior and help lead the way experimentally to better patterns of living.

But even when men recognize the same ideals, they frequently fall out over methods. The end goals can be the same, but the methods may affect different individuals differently. Hence there may be an honest difference of opinion about the reasonableness and equity of various possible methods.

Here again there is an over-all method that has universal applicability. Within its framework, the more specific methods can find their appropriate spheres. If the over-all pattern is kept firmly in view, co-operation on details becomes possible.

This method or pattern is the democratic way of life. Democracy as a principle, and applied realistically, meets the tests of equity, flexibility, and freedom, in serving the purposes of society and in meeting the needs of the individual as defined in Chapters III and IV. It offers the best chance for the individual to develop fully, consistent with group advancement. Democracy is essentially a method of harmonizing individual and group conflicts and of harnessing the total efforts of individuals working singly and of society as a whole. Individual and social objectives are often in apparent conflict, but in reality the greatest human happiness comes only as these objectives are harmonized and unified in action.

Man is not wholly like the lion—aloof, selfish, predatory in his habits—nor does his society resemble the swarm of bees with its closely knit, interdependent fabric. He is similar to each in that he is both an individual and a social being. Each individual adds his contributions to the total of social strength and values, and is in turn dependent upon the group as a whole. Modern society, particularly, is infinitely complex and interrelated. In spite of discords, it has essential and necessary unity. But within this social fabric, each individual desires and needs relative freedom to follow his personal inclinations and to pursue his own activities.

Looked at in this light, the weakness of extreme individualism as a form of social organization becomes apparent. Suitable to pioneer and frontier conditions, where self-sufficiency is at a premium, and exploitation is the predominant method, individualism breaks down when economic interdependence forces men to live with greater regard for the rights, and in greater subservience to the productive efforts, of others. Collectivism, too, in its extreme form, has serious disadvantages. The society which has no other end than the social one, and which accordingly subordinates the individual to the group, refuses to recognize the most valuable and valued possession of men—the distinctive personality of each. It is man's precious gift that each individual is unlike every other. Each person has existing and potential characteristics which only he possesses; each has talents peculiar to himself which when developed enable him to express himself in a distinctive way. But the highly collectivist state, as it has revealed itself in practice, limits freedom of movement, expression, and action, suppresses experimental endeavor, prescribes dogmatic beliefs, and generally warps the personalities of its individual members.

It is because of the advantage which it offers in striving for the maximum of individual and social effectiveness that democracy meets the test as the best way of life man has yet conceived. Where individualism loses group advantages because of the anarchy of the individual, and collectivism suppresses the personality of the individual, democracy constantly experiments to find the point of harmony through which the greatest total advantages can come. Thus is individual freedom preserved at the same time that social aims are achieved. Indeed, the kind of restriction on freedom which this implies is often the very means by which can be accomplished those social purposes which in turn give to the individual the maximum opportunity for his personal advancement.

The basic principle inherent in the democratic way is applicable on the world scale. Here is posed a similar problem—harmonizing and harnessing the objectives and efforts of individual geographical and racial groups for the general welfare of the people of the world as a whole. The individual nation craves recognition, respect, and prosperity. But modern communication and economic development have made of the world a complex social organism; future progress can come only through co-operation of all groups or nations toward common objectives. Nations must therefore surrender their claim to do as they please. Democracy as applied on a world basis means the development of a new world-order with the dual goal of cultural autonomy and economic co-operation, and with sufficient political integration to achieve this end.

This argument does not imply that we have all of the necessary knowledge or adequate intelligence with which to reform the world overnight. The point is that we do have a fine inheritance of knowledge, we understand the techniques by which to increase that knowledge, and we have gained confidence in the experimental approach toward the solution of our problems. There is a certain satisfaction in working in an imperfect world: it makes striving toward perfection both possible and fruitful.

We come, then, to the question: Education for what? Education for cultured gentlemen—with its implication of class distinctions, and of elegant leisure? Education to transmit the cultural heritage—with the focus on the past and the tendency to cling to the *status quo*? Education to produce rounded individuals—for what purpose? Education for life —without indicating what kind of life is the goal?

Perhaps the ultimate objective contains some elements of all of these. For we can use educated gentlemen, in the better sense. We need the wisdom produced by the cultural heritage. We want individuals educated in a well-rounded way. We ought to have the main focus of education on contemporary life. But we should go beyond these criteria of what education is for. We need to educate for the good life.

What the good life is must be determined experimentally; at any given time it is relative to all past life. For the present, many of us are convinced that the ideal of democracy represents the best life yet conceived. If so, it is the responsibility of education to help bring the democratic way of life to fuller realization.

The assumption that man is in the last analysis able to bring both his personality and his society to greater perfection indicates that education has a vital role to play. Especially in a democratic society is education both the instrument for making democracy possible and for achieving the larger individual and social values. If democracy is the method of intelligence in action for the social group as a whole, education is the key to defining and constructing it. Democracy, then, is the medium in which intelligence can become freed and put to work. Education is the specific channel through which intelligence is released; through which aptitudes, talents, and interests are discovered; and through which knowledge is acquired and accumulated, the power to think increased and disciplined, skills of expression and action learned, and the personality generally cultivated and refined. In the educational institution, also, lies the opportunity to explore for new knowledge and new methods, to speculate upon possible new goals, to formulate new ideals, and to help determine future social direction. Thus can evolution based upon intelligence be substituted for revolution based upon force.

INDEX

Ds

FRANKLIN AND MARSHALL COLLEGE
LB2321 .H4   010101 000
Henderson, Algo Donmyer,
Vitalizing liberal education.

0 1114 00409038